SEASONS AMONG THE VINES

SEASONS AMONG THE VINES

Life Lessons
from the
California
Wine Country
and Paris

*Paula
Moulton*

SHE WRITES PRESS

Published 2013

Printed in the United States of America

ISBN: 978-1-938314-16-2

Library of Congress Control Number: 2013953910

For information, address:

She Writes Press

1563 Solano Ave #546

Berkeley, CA 94707

For Stephen,
with love

In water one sees one's own face;
But in wine one beholds the heart of another.
—French Proverb

CONTENTS

Spring

Summer

A NOTE FROM THE FARMER

I'm a city-girl-gone-country whose love affair with farming brought me to Glen Ellen, California, to take up a venture I could've only jumped into with the enthusiasm of someone who doesn't quite know what she's getting herself into. For me, grapevines are celebrated weeds much in the way diamonds are treasured rocks. (Indulge me, please. Farming requires a definite, if weird, sense of humor.) This book is an invitation to the reader—nature enthusiast, food and wine lover, bold women and men, backyard gardener, and even those who've never thought about farming—to learn a thing or two about grape-growing and winemaking. Browse—or study—the sidebars interspersed throughout the narrative for interesting facts; you'll learn that growing grapes can be as simple as cultivating weeds, and making wine can be done by just about anyone (the former by those without a green thumb and the latter by those without a culinary degree). You can do this practically anywhere—whether you live in the suburbs of Berkeley or the high-rises of Manhattan. When you open a bottle of wine produced from grapes stomped upon by your family and friends, from fruit lovingly grown on grapevines (weeds) you tended, I predict that your neighbors will talk—wherever they live—and they'll be green with envy.

INTRODUCTION TO
THE NEW EDITION

A flash of memories from the past ten years leaps through my mind as I stoop to wipe up the spilled wine from the floor. Here I am on June 1 of 2012 in my last wine management exam at Le Cordon Bleu School. I am one of twenty students from fourteen different countries, and I have just splattered red wine all over the two French judges. I thought stuff like this only happened in the movies.

My year in Paris leading up to this moment has been filled with adventures, but mostly those experiences have been within the confines of the classroom. My French professor held our attention for many long days of enology and winemaking. Although we had a British translator, I can only begin to imagine what was lost in translation. This was exhausting to experience in a classroom. Still, there was untold camaraderie between Monsieur Ramage, our professor, and BP, the British translator. The way they bantered back and forth in English and French held me captive and entertained for ten long months.

Three weeks into our ten-month course, we were told that we must write in French on all our exams. Those first weeks were grueling. We had to learn about French harvesting and winemaking, plus French vocabulary. Each of us was also assigned a month-long internship, during which we would live with French families that owned and ran wineries throughout southwest France. I had no idea how I would survive speaking only French and helping to run a winery, especially with my lack of French language skills. I wondered more than a few times if I had made a big mistake in leaving my fiancé and children and coming to Paris.

Still, my ten months in Paris proved to be one of best experiences of my life. Besides the many hours a week spent in class, my year was filled with wine adventures that began with that first internship, where I worked as a cellar rat in Bergerac, followed a few months later by an internship as a sommelier at a restaurant, Citrus Etoile, off the Champs Elysees. Later, I worked with a British filmmaker and a classmate, a former BBC journalist, on a two-week project that involved traveling throughout the country to interview the brightest and boldest winemakers and sommeliers of France.

Among those flashes of memories that pass through my head while I contemplate the consequences of splattering red wine on my judges and failing my wine course is the catastrophic moment that changed my life, which ultimately led me to this ancient building in Paris's 15th arrondissement in the first place.

It's true what they say about life's precariousness. It can change in an instant—and mine did. Ten years ago, I described myself as a city-girl-gone-country because I was a San Franciscan who moved to Sonoma, California, to become a wine grape farmer. To a lot of people, the word *farmer* conjures up images of a man dressed in dungarees with a piece of hay dangling from the side of his mouth as words like "darn," "dangit," and "little missus" slip from his tongue. I never fit that picture, or even aspired to. Instead, after long days of tending my sixty acres of land, I did things like raise money for charitable causes and hold events where I danced in an evening gown and a pair of sexy stilettos. But still, I owned a farm that I cultivated with my own manicured hands.

My passion for wine grape farming kept me happy for years. I loved my life in Sonoma, raising my three children in a blissfully happy marriage and working on my sixty acres. This was where I was when I set out to write *Seasons Among the Vines* in 2003.

Just days before the book was released, however, my husband Chuck was killed in a head-on car crash. Instead of attending my first scheduled book signing, I attended Chuck's funeral. That weekend, my children and I shifted from secure and happy people to a devastated and grieving family. Chuck's crash lead to a slew of exorbitantly expensive lawsuits, and so with one brief and tragic incident, the sixty acres of land, most of our personal possessions, my wine career, and worst of all, our happiness, were stolen away.

The curtain dropped on my life, and all I saw for the next five years was darkness. Along with the bleak ugliness of lawsuits and the loss of our land and possessions, we suffered the deception of some of our closest friends. Through it all, my three children—Ashley, who was sixteen when Chuck died; Christopher, who was thirteen; and Alexandra, who was ten—and I stuck together and supported one another. We held on to our love and respect for one another despite our grieving hearts and jumbled souls. No one could break our bond or take that away. And this is how we remain today. Even though we were left with a broken world and no plan for our future, we refused to give up.

I am no longer a city-girl-gone-country; instead, I've temporarily become a country-girl-gone-city. I am in Paris now, and my enrollment in the wine management program is part leap of faith, part adventure, and part pushing the envelope. I've come here to learn everything I can about the international world of wine: terroir, the growing practices of other countries, the thousands of grape varieties that I didn't know, and most of all, how to smell, swirl, and taste some of the finest wines of the world. But I've also come to Paris to dust off emotional grime, shake up my life a bit, and self-reflect.

My youngest daughter and I received acceptance letters on the same day in early spring of 2011; hers was from Cornell University, and mine was from the pilot program of wine management at Le Cordon Bleu in Paris. Unlike Alexandra's future classmates, the twenty students in my class would range in age from twenty-two to sixty, and most of us would be the only representative of our native countries (Turkey, Finland, Brazil, Russia, Scotland, England, America, Korea, Singapore, China, Kazakhstan, and more).

Today, the second day of our two days of final exams, the classroom is much like a stage. I am not a star, however, since I've just "wall-papered" the French judges—that is, I have just uncorked the bottle during my traditional decanting procedure, and because of heat and pressure within the bottle, the expulsion of the cork caused the red wine to spatter, dousing the judges before I was able to methodically decant and pour the wine into their glasses. I realize at this moment that I have most likely failed this portion of my five-part oral exam. "How did I get here?" I mutter to myself. I am kneeling with my back facing the judges, wiping the mess from the floor.

But rather than grovel to the judges about what my last ten months have been like, I stand up straight and decide that I must face them and hold my head high with dignity.

The two judges, one man and one woman, wear light-colored summer business attire. The other students, like me, are dressed in formal black suits with the silver Cordon Bleu pin attached to our left lapels. The judges' cold stares cut through me. To avoid their hostile glares, I grab a napkin from the box labeled "serviettes" lying on the floor next to my wine mess and contemplate wiping up the droplets of wine dripping down the nose of the male judge. I feel as silly as Inspector Clouseau bumbling his way through a *Pink Panther* movie.

The other students all still carry a tray in their left hands. The trays are each filled with two saucers, two wine glasses and a tasting glass, a match, a candle set on a tippy stand, and two black napkins folded neatly atop one another. In their right hands they carry an empty decanter. The weather is a sweltering 98 degrees Fahrenheit, and it is the first day of smothering heat and glowing sunshine we have had in nearly seven months. We all have black circles under our eyes from lack of sun and vitamin D deficiency. And I am tired beyond any fatigue that I can ever remember in my life.

I was required to eloquently perform the twenty-six steps necessary for proper, traditional French red wine decanting. Never mind the fact that I have completed a six-hour comprehensive written final and waltzed through four of my academic orals sputtering jargon about the French AOCs (*appellation d'origine controlee*—the "controlled designation of origin," and how this pertains to the geographical limits and rules of French winemaking), world terroirs, international wine prices, and everything one could imagine about the countless varietals and regions of the wine world.

But after all of this, in the midst of the twenty-six steps, I "wallpapered" the judges, and that is one of the all-time worst things a trained wine specialist/sommelier could ever do.

My heart was broken when Chuck was killed, and it was all I could do to keep my children on track. I wanted to go to the heart doctor and demand that he find the hole in my chest; instead, I focused on the things I needed to do to protect my children's future. I got out of bed each day, swung my feet onto the cold floor, and studied them briefly, just to remind myself that they were really mine and that this really was my life. For months this ceremony prompted me to stay connected to myself and my world, and it made me feel empowered and safe, the way I remembered feeling when I perceived that I had some sort of control over my life--whether that perception was an illusion or not. Only my responsibility for my three kids kept me alive during those hardest years and enabled me to muster the energy I needed to continue on.

I was terrified to learn about who I really was and about moving on with my life. For many years, I lived in two worlds—one real and one unreal. I no longer believed there was a dividing line between heaven and earth. I fought this notion daily, but I couldn't overcome my suspicion that some hole or doorway or bridge existed that would open the lines of communication between the dead and the living. Although I knew that Chuck was not alive, I did not accept it, and this lead me to believe that I could bring him back.

My dreams had a new meaning after Chuck's death because that was where he and I communicated each night. For months I'd awaken with my face wet, covered with my own tears. I had a recurring dream in which the phone would ring, and on the other line Chuck would say, "I'm hurrying to get home to you. Just be patient." It was always the same British phone booth, bright red and surrounded by heavy white fog. We would discuss how to turn back time, and there were many months that I believed we really could figure it out so that he could come home to me.

But now ten years have passed, and Chuck never did come home. The decade I spent concerned only with self-preservation and the preservation of my three children is over, and with its end came the time to finally fulfill my aspirations, hopes, and goals. I realized it is now my moment to triumph by going back to pursuing my dreams.

※ ※ ※

After I lost my land, my yearning to grow and produce the perfect wine grape evolved. I wanted to acquire land again, to continue to maintain healthy soil and practice organic farming, but now I also wanted to expand my knowledge of the art of winemaking and delve further into the secrets of food and wine pairing as it relates to the practice of choosing, cooking, and eating good food and wine—the true art of fine gastronomy. It was the unleashing of these desires that landed me in Paris, France, in the first place, the hub of beauty and elegance and home to a culture of experts in the art of traditional gastronomy and old-world winemaking.

It doesn't take me long to understand how important tradition is to the French, especially where their food and wine are concerned, and yet I have an unsettling belief that tradition is not what we should base our choices on when it comes to food and wine. My first month here, I learn that my ultimate goal will be to challenge the code of traditional food and wine pairing as if I am a technically trained ballerina branching out into the freedom and artistic creativity of a modern dancer. I want to be an innovator and extend the limits of food and wine pairing by stretching the boundaries of tradition.

Although I will always view myself as a farmer, my desire now is to teach the wine consumer how to feel confident, be adventurous, and lose the intimidation factor when it comes to choosing wine. My greatest wish is to give you, the reader—whether you're an aspiring wine critic or even a full-fledged winey—the knowledge and the tools you need to play with the biggest and boldest wine critics, even the French. After all, wine is about pleasure, and what could be more pleasurable than feeling confident and free when it comes to choosing a wine?

Fall

God made only water, but man made wine.
—Victor Hugo, Les Contemplations

FALL IN PARIS

2011

*W*ine is a food. I never understood this concept until I arrived in France and sat down to many meals waiting to be served a lovely French wine aperitif. The French don't drink wine as an aperitif unless, of course, it's served with hors d'oeuvres. This was my first introduction to tradition and my first glimpse at just how different American and French gastronomy is. The main difference is that Americans view wine as a beverage to drink at any time, regardless of whether it's paired with food or not, while the French find this distasteful; to them it's like eating a hot dog without a bun.

As with food, wine is a potpourri of scents. I love that a certain smell can evoke memories of summer; or that a spicy aroma can bring me back to my childhood and the warmth of the holiday season; or that a musty smell can remind me of the times my friends and I would jump into piles of leaves after the first fall rain. Hidden in the domain of scents lies the gateway to our own personal scent libraries, and those libraries can evoke memories that we've often forgotten.

As I sit in class on the second day of school, all I can smell is the stale air of a room filled with too many students. There are no windows, and there's not enough space to house all of us comfortably. It is September 2011 in Paris, and the streets are filled with tourists and locals sitting at outdoor cafes, sipping cool drinks and lounging in the glorious weather. But I hurried past them on my way to class this morning, remembering that the purpose of my time in this city lies here, on the second floor of Le Cordon Bleu, in an old windowless storage room once used for cooking supplies, utensils, and towels that is now our classroom.

The lesson beginning today—one that will continue to be a life-long challenge even for a crackerjack wine expert—is focused on unlocking the most important elements in wine: aromas. Once we learn this, we not only will be able to describe the key elements of a particular wine, but we will feel confident about openly engaging in communication and thought with other wine lovers and foodies. We will ultimately be able to choose the wines best suited to certain foods, seasons, and our own and others' unique palates.

A giant red box labeled *Le Nez du Vin* stands on the desk at the front of the room, and our teacher wears a grin across his face. Months later I will finally understand that Monsieur Ramage's smile is based on his sheer excitement and passion at being able to expose his first international students to the meaning of wine. "The old adage 'You can't teach an old dog new tricks' does not pertain to our sense of smell," he says. "It's never too late to uncover the mystique of new aromas and to add them to one's memory."

* * *

The first key in being a winey is to play the aroma memory game and do it well. The *Le Nez du Vin* box is filled with fifty-four vials of aromas. *Le Nez du Vin* is the brainchild of genius Jean Lenoir, a Burgundy-born wine expert whose invention has helped people worldwide to learn the scents needed to properly describe wine aromas. Our goal at this first attempt with *Le Nez du Vin* is to take two sniffs from each vial, determine its scent, and jot down what it is quickly before moving on to the other fifty-three vials. Is it truffle, mushroom, smoke, vanilla, acacia, green pepper, grapefruit, orange, or rose?

I spend ten months shopping my way through Parisian stores discretely picking up and smelling fruits, vegetables, and flowers simply to memorize and hold their smells in my scent library for future use in wine analysis. No one is born with a perfect wine palate, and since we don't learn how to smell in school, this is where the entertainment and mastery of understanding wine begins—your rose garden, your neighbor's acacia tree, or even your local grocery store.

I am a neophyte at the game of smelling when I start my first internship in Bergerac. The harvest won't wait, and part of this internship is about experiencing firsthand what goes on with harvesting, winemaking, bottling, and labeling.

I discover that my education in aromas and smell is not halted by my internship in Bergerac, but rather is complemented by those four weeks of arduous winery work. Smelling aromas from vials in the classroom is one way to identify wine once it reaches the glass, but those scents pale in comparison to the true mystery of wine aromas that actually begin in the vineyard.

Where do wine aromas come from? I consider the smells of grapes, and ultimately wine, to be one of the greatest miracles of nature. Each spring, grapes begin their yearly cycle with budburst. As the shoots grow and flowers bloom, their floral aromas develop; however, during berry development, veraison, and early ripening, the seeds become enveloped in a protection system that blocks their aroma until they are fully ripe. Once the grapes are ripe, an enzyme that is composed of protein within the grape berry becomes active and produces a reaction that releases an abundance of aromas.

All of these aroma-producing processes are broken down into three aroma classifications: primary, secondary, and tertiary. In simple terms, the primary aromas come from the variety of grape, the terroir, the climate, the soil, and the farmer's management of the grapevine. A grapevine grown around pine trees may have a hint of pine aroma in the finished wine, while a grapevine grown near the ocean may produce wines that are salty and remind us of the beach. Wines can actually produce the aromas of the land where they are grown, and this is where their primary smells come from.

The secondary aromas are inspired by the fermentation process. Primary fermentation is generally three to five days long and occurs after the grapes are crushed when natural yeast or added yeast consumes the sugar and converts it into alcohol and carbon dioxide. Secondary fermentation is a slower process that lasts about one to three weeks and is the final conversion of sugar to alcohol. The fermentation process induces a transformation of the grape that produces esters, alcohols, and aldehydes, which add to the wine's aromatic components. By-products like ethyl butanoate, an ester, can produce a pineapple note, while ethyl 3-methylbutanoate, also an ester, can produce an apple note. Some wines also go through malolactic fermentation, the transformation of malic into lactic acids, which produces diacetyl or butanedione and creates a buttery aroma.

Finally, there are the tertiary aromas, which come from the maturing and aging processes of the wine. Was it aged in oak barrels, or did it remain in stainless steel? The most commonly produced aroma from an oak barrel is vanilla, but other aromas found in this third process include leather, mushroom, almond, smoke, and coffee.

I try to process my job here in Bergerac as a cellar rat and make sense out of how my work relates to becoming an expert in wine, and specifically in aromas. "Cellar rat," in wine terms, is a person who does odd jobs (or in my case, *all* jobs) at a winery. That includes everything from harvesting, punching down, pumping over, doing temperature analysis of fermenting must, cleaning winery equipment, and bottling and labeling.

Punching down and pumping over, or *remontage* in French, is done twice a day while fermentation is occurring. During the conversion process of sugar to alcohol, a cap of skins, seeds, and pulp is formed over the top of the juice in the tanks. The cap must be "punched down," or broken up each day and stirred into the juice. Then the juice from the bottom of the tank must be drawn up and "pumped over," or put back into the top of the tank to be stirred in and to help break up the cap. This allows the process of fermentation to continue. If the cap is left untouched, the fermentation process will stop and bacteria will form, and you will end up with vinegar and not wine. The process also helps to increase the extraction of color, tannin, and flavors from the grapes.

One day during the internship, two of us cellar rats are sent off to help the neighbors with their bottling. Since it is now late fall, harvest is almost complete for the winemaker we are working for, and we are excited to do something other than pick grapes with the fifteen gypsy women this vineyard employs. The Bergerac region produces some sweet wines from Botrytis cinerea grapes—grapes that are affected by a gray fungus or noble rot, which sucks the water out of the berries, concentrates the sugars, and magnifies the sweetness and complexity of the wine—and this produces some of the most desirable and enchanting sweet dessert wines of France. Our days of harvesting Semillon grapes consist of sticky hands, hair filled with flies, and the overpowering primary aromas of honey and sweet melon that become so prevalent in a finished sauterne wine.

I've never seen a portable bottling machine. The one the neighbors rent is tucked inside a moveable trailer that is rigged to a large truck. It doesn't look very stable, but I am instructed to hop up on it and get busy unloading empty bottles onto the assembly line that will move the bottles through, fill them with wine from the tanks outside, cork them, and line them up at the end. After only an hour of this I am well trained and ready to never do this again, but we have a long day ahead.

The machine backs up a few times during the day, and all I hear from the screaming bottling driver is, "*Appuyez sur le bouton rouge, maintenant!*" (Press on the red button, now!) It's one of those days when I feel a bit like a deer in the headlights. It's too much effort to understand everything being said around me. I try anyway, though I can base my decision as to whether I'll push the red stop button by the sheer anger of the bottling man alone.

My classmate and I are like Lucy and Ethel in an *I Love Lucy* episode. We are dressed with scarves around our necks, trendy boots, and city raincoats just in case it gets cold and rainy. Short of a miracle, I am not sure how I will get through this day. The bottling captain is discouraged by our lack of skills.

Twenty-five thousand bottles later, we are still loading empty bottles onto the conveyor belt. The sun has gone down, and the clanging sounds of the bottles rattle my brain. I feel like my whole body is shaking from the vibration of the noise and the bouncing of the bottles as they bobble down the track on their way to the five spigots.

"Oh fuck," my classmate says. Some of the bottles have fallen off the pallet and banged to the ground. She is stuck kneeling on top of six pallets nearly ten feet off the ground, from which she has been handing me bottles to load onto the conveyor, so I jump off the trailer and start grabbing the rolling bottles. But this starts a chain reaction, and eventually some of the bottles knock the trailer just enough to stop the assembly line of upright bottles as they make their way to the spigots. The attendant comes running and begins yelling obscenities I don't understand. "We've done it now," I tell her. We are exhausted after hours of work, and neither of us cares anymore.

I decide I probably don't make a great cellar rat. Standing amidst the jumble of bottles, I flashback to the morning when three other female classmates—one French, one Turkish, and one Finish—and I took over the pumping-over duties for our out-of-town winery owner. Two of us were perched on the tank, and two ran the pump and held the hose. But before too long, we lost control of the hose and sprayed fermenting Malbec all over the walls and floor of the pristine winery. The secondary aromas of that mess were abruptly halted with our error. The smooth process of fermentation was disrupted, and because of that, the clove and cinnamon aromas that may have ensued were not able to develop. As I again stoop to gather more runaway bottles, I realize that my internship to date is probably more punctuated by mistakes than successes.

The bottling machine finally starts up again, and I am ready. I have the bottles lined up on the conveyor belt. The owner of the winery and his wife show up and grab a bottle midway through the filling cycle, visually summing up our empty pallets. I hope this means that we are finished for the day; instead, the bottle is passed to each of us for a sniff and a swig. I find this sharing ritual utterly insane when I see them put the bottle back on the assembly line and watch it move toward the spigot to be refilled.

I envision some American picking up this bottle in a U.S. wine store, examining this old-world wine coming from the Bergerac region of France, and innocently buying this bottle, ignorant of our tasting. Is this quality control? Everyone smiles and talks about the perfection of this Merlot with its black cherry, chocolate, spice, and hints of leather. The wine is now a combination of primary, secondary, and tertiary aromas, and it's a masterful compilation of all three elements.

Standing in this open field, in fall, on a bottling trailer attached to a truck filled with a twenty-five-foot-long bottling machine, I realize that I have traded commercialization and inspections for rustic innocence. The smells of autumn will forever evoke memories of the month I spent in Bergerac as a cellar rat, and most of all, the uncanny day I spent on the bottling line smelling the inexplicable beauty and potpourri of yellowed grasses, dried lavender, and musty leaves. Most of all, though, it will represent the freedom I felt in surviving those first few months away from my homeland.

ONE

A CLUSTER OFF THE OLD VINE

2003

*I*n Sonoma wine country, the smells of fall are rich, the air damp and musty. Tourists flock to the valley like children stalking an elusive butterfly, and they stroll through the spellbinding wine towns breathing in the delicious bouquet and inhaling the splendid aromas. Sometimes, if they're lucky, they get a chance to converse with a famous winemaker who might be taking a quick lunch break away from the frenetic pace of harvest. But the most powerful part of our fall season is how the smells make the farmer feel. The pungent scents release feelings of elation and uneasiness; elation from knowing you made it successfully through a year of farming, uneasiness from having to let go of something you have poured your heart and soul into for an entire year.

There's also an energy in the atmosphere that can't be explained. The tourists can feel it, too. They come to witness this electrifying vitality—sipping wine and watching the natives busy themselves with picking grapes and crushing fruit. One can saunter down the street at night and view the buzz of the wineries no matter what time it is: the music is blaring, winery workers are laughing, and everyone is acting as if there is no need to sleep. There is a profoundly intoxicating aura that hypnotizes not just the out-of-town guests, but the natives as well.

After many years of living in the wine country, I've learned that even though every season in farming seems to bring everlasting infatuation abundant with Promethean ideas, hardships, and new-fangled lessons, fall is a time of fresh, hopeful beginnings and a brief juncture where I can start over. It's the time to shrug off the past year's mistakes and make amends for my most recent growing failures; it's the moment to enthusiastically chart a new course for becoming a better farmer and an interlude when I can reflect upon the hard-earned knowledge that I've acquired. It's also the time to soak up the last rays of the calming summer sun, take in all the aromatic scents of crush, and romanticize about the future.

My tale starts in the fall because it's the season my family loves the most, and because it was fall when we first moved to the country. When we arrived at our farm ten years ago, my kids were just six, four, and two. I surprised them by erecting a giant, canvas teepee in the front yard. Grace, Dude, and Joy were ecstatic. Placed no more than twenty feet away from our rows of berry-filled grapevines, it stood nearly fifteen feet high, painted with brightly colored animals and dancing Native Americans. Dude saw it first, "Wow, Mom!" he screamed, flashing his toothless grin. "Can we sleep in it? Please? Pretty please!" The girls were happy, too. And nevermind the house just yet, I thought to myself, although it was spectacular with its ivy-enveloped stone front, and its arbors covered with prolific wisteria and fragrant star jasmine. The teepee was meant to take my children's gaze away from the vast acres of land that might make them feel isolated and overwhelmed. I'd worried that their new home would seem over-powering and frightening and much like being lost in a national forest. But the teepee standing in the open field surrounded by twinkling oak meadows and rows of brilliant fruiting vines made us all feel like we had just nailed the best camping spot in a park over-crowded with nature lovers. As it would turn out, I was the one in store for a culture shock; my children loved their new home.

I had a dream inherent—or rather a nightmare—that first night we spent in the country. It was like one of those horrible, sweat-filled dreams where you're the center of attention and everyone is laughing and pointing and you don't know why. The dream had that gut-wrenching effect of ridicule, ignorance, panic, and self-doubt. The message was there: I was in over my head living my new life as a farmer.

In the beginning, my weeds—the seven acres of spirited grapevines I acquired by mortgaging my life away—were in need of care by someone who knew more about farming than I did. And no sooner had I passed through the gates of our twenty-four acres of deer-fenced property did I realize I hadn't a clue about how to manage the eight-year-old grapevines we'd inherited. I simply had not accumulated enough knowledge from the quick reading I had done before we packed our things and left the city. The anxiety associated with making a mistake frustrated me. It was as if my vines were nasty children I couldn't control.

* * *

Somehow I would have to acquire at least some of the skills that my established, old-time Sonoma neighbor-farmers already had. Many of them came from generations of farming people, while I had only my strong motivation and some technical knowledge I had acquired from reading a couple of viticulture textbooks. When I confronted Chuck with my doubts and fears, he came up with a viable suggestion:

"Why don't you go back to school and study grape-growing?" he said. This suggestion eventually turned into one full year, forty hours a week, of studying about grapes and winemaking. There was a lot to learn then, and a lot to learn now.

Viticulture, the study of how to grow grapes, was a popular subject among farmers, mostly male farmers at that time, who wanted to exchange their crops for more lucrative crops like grapes, and among would-be farmers like myself (also mostly male) who wanted to take a stab at pursuing grape-growing as a new career.

So before I knew it, I was enrolled, full-time, in classes on everything a commercial farmer would need to know about how to grow grapes. The first two classes I registered for dealt with how to operate tractors (the treasured tool of farmers) and soil analysis. The soil class was no problem, but tractor class was another story.

When I walked into the classroom at Santa Rosa Junior College on the first day of viticulture school, it wasn't what I'd expected. Unlike any lecture room I'd experienced, there was dirt and grass on the floor and lots of men wearing plaid shirts, wrangler jeans, and muddy boots. My thoughts flashed on the stereotypes I had held long ago about farmers. The professor wore the same attire as the rest of the students, and he had a slow, country drawl which, surprisingly, relaxed me; I felt immediately intrigued. I'd never had a teacher that seemed so untroubled on the first day of class. He wasn't busily scribbling jargon on a giant chalkboard; instead, he was cheerily conversing with a few of the guys sitting in the front row. I heard them talking enthusiastically about inseminating cows, new and improved pig feeds, and how to put shoes on a belligerent horse. Could I ever be like them, have that kind of knowledge about those types of things? I took a seat in the back of the room hoping to blend in with the group.

As he began his lecture about the benefits of grape-growing, I am certain that many of the students wondered what I was doing there among all those energetic male farmers. I wondered myself. It reminded me of my first job after college when I arrived for work and all of my co-workers were men—men who had formed a strong camaraderie from working together for years. Would I ever be a "chip off the old block?" Not here, that was for sure. There were no farmers that I knew of—male or female—in my family. Sitting in that classroom at Santa Rosa Junior College I experienced that feeling of all eyes on me, everyone wondering if I'd pull my weight and be able to tough it out. This time, though, I was ready for a challenge. I didn't feel ill at ease or intimated; this time I felt empowered. Time had given me omnipotence and the strength to understand that I was following my dream, and I would carry through with those things that were most important to me—no matter how much I stuck out.

But because my city upbringing had not provided me with tractor finesse, and I knew absolutely nothing about how to use one, I found the curriculum on how to purchase, drive, and maintain a tractor extremely difficult. In fact, my worst grade in viticulture school came from tractor class. While I struggled to learn the basic engine parts, my classmates, enthusiastic younger-than-me men who had spent their youth dabbling in tractors, cars, and whatever other machinery they could locate around the family farm, breezed through the material. I'm of the mind that vehicles of all sorts are a means to an end, and I took no satisfaction from learning how the actual machinery functioned.

My first tractor exam took place in a vacant room filled with three large tables on which lay pieces of every imaginable part of a tractor, disassembled and scattered randomly about. The goal was to identify each part and write the correct name in the corresponding blank space on the test paper. It was like biology class in high school when we dissected frogs and I labeled three of the organs with "liver" because they all looked like the liver my mother used to make us eat. Who was I kidding? How could I cope with these metal objects that lay before me?

I panicked when I looked down at my test results and realized that my answer to five of the questions read "fuel filter."

"Shasta," I said to the student standing next to me, "I'm never gonna make it through this." I had the sense of mind to know that one tractor would not possess five fuel filters. Like an ill-prepared law student floundering for words during a mock classroom trial, I dug through my tractor vocabulary searching for creative words to fill in the blanks. They were imaginative all right.

To this day I thank those boys who jabbed me in the ribs with the ends of their pencils and shook their heads in disbelief when they glimpsed my test paper. Luckily, their contorted faces and flapping eyelids managed to wake me up and forced me to push a little deeper into my memory. Somehow, with their assistance, I managed to dig up some fresh mechanical terminology that proved to fit those cold metal pieces that lay before me.

I may have been among the least safe of the students who was finally allowed to mount the tractors, which felt a little like mounting a horse: you need to exercise the same care in flinging yourself over the top without causing yourself to fly off the other side. A true farmer instinctively knows the correct amount of energy it takes to do this. I, on the other hand, had to pour all of my concentration into looking as if I had been doing this my whole life. As we stood in a chilly barn on that very first day of class, the tractor instructor pointed in my direction and snapped, "You—get on the tractor and move it out of the barn." I nearly choked. Could he really mean me? As I turned around to see if the guy behind me was moving to carry out his order, the instructor briskly stomped his booted foot and pointed his finger directly at me. He bellowed, "No! I am talking to you, Missy. Come here and move 'er out!" Sure that he was picking on me because I was the only female, I begrudgingly walked toward the massive tractor trying to muster up the confidence I felt everyone expected.

I wanted to scream out in indignation, Who the hell are you calling "missy" anyway? I wanted to kick him where it hurt with my

27

coveted pink cowboy boots that I bought shortly after moving to the country. But knowing full well that this would wipe out my chances of ever gaining the respect of the rest of the farmers in the class, not to mention that it would earn me the first "F" of my life, I gritted my teeth and held on to my anger. My fragile-looking feminine stride scared him, I'm sure, as I swayed my way up to the tractor. Clearly he doubted my ability to carry out his order, but I sensed his doubt and it challenged me to rise to the occasion to make him swallow whatever disdain he hoped to feel at seeing me fail. It took every ounce of pride and fortitude I had to ignore his tough cowboy demeanor and not make up an excuse about why I felt another classmate would be better suited to the task. The last thing I wanted to do was compromise my dream because I was embarrassed about accomplishing something, and because I was concerned about being someone who wasn't what others thought I should be.

I felt myself start to tremble and stopped myself cold, wondering the whole time what the consequences would be if I accidentally removed a barn wall or ran over a classmate's foot while I moved this giant heap of metal out of the dark barn and into the sunlight. I was fighting to prove myself; but more than that I felt like I was fighting for men's respect of women worldwide—a lofty image to pull me through. As I climbed on with my calculated mount, I told myself not to fail simply because of my inability to accept the fact that I might be successful. I had to stop hiding behind my competence. There were nearly twenty men watching with bated breath.

Feigning total confidence, as if I had not a problem in the world, I held my head high, flicked my unloosed hair out of my face, and entered into the sunlight. I could hear hesitant applause arising from the barn behind me. I let out a sigh of relief with the knowledge that there was at least a glimmer of hope that some of those guys actually wanted me to succeed. I didn't have to hide in the back corner of the barn all semester, or worse yet, forever be a passenger on the backside of the tractor. I could be in the driver's seat without anyone giving me orders.

That first day of tractor class seemed like the longest day of my life. Not only did I have to take the mechanical test and move the tractor out of the barn, but afterwards all the students had to cultivate a small piece of acreage into a baseball field. The tractor instructor disappeared briefly just after my first (and only) large vehicle "show," and before I knew it he had spun the tractor around masterfully, coming to a halt in front of me while the rest of the class was assembling outside the barn. I think it was his attempt to prove that he could certainly outmaneuver me on the tractor, and I wasn't challenging that.

Once he had the rest of the students' attention, he was off, whipping down the vineyard rows as the fierce sun beat down onto his face, laughing and gesturing at the wildness of the three-hundred-something acres of college-owned farmland, a portion of which we were going to tame. At that moment, the wildness resided not in the land but in his excitement. He planned to create a playing field out of the raw, unkempt earth, and he looked carefree and joyful as he immersed himself and us in the project ahead. I wanted to share his energy and witness the same beauty he saw, even though the field looked more like a huge weed patch rather than a pristine baseball area. I wanted to feel what he felt and I wanted to believe that all I would need for this was to mount my own Kubota tractor and fly through the rows of my vineyard with the demeanor of a true farmer.

We finished that playing field after a long, hot eight-hour day of swapping two school-owned tractors among twenty students, each of us taking thirty-minute shifts. Our faces were scorched and our bodies were covered with a fine layer of dust that turned into dark droplets of sweat as the day wore on.

As the hours of that day skipped by I decided to come to terms with the title of "Missy," so eloquently awarded me by my tractor professor. I decided to treat it as a rite of passage and view it as serving a higher cause. After all, wasn't it I who had earned the respect of my colleagues, guys who were patting me on the back as we took our turns on the tractor. Better than that, some of them even wanted to talk to me about some of the moves I had done, wanted to swap maneuvers with a complete rookie. For being one of the longest days of my life, it was certainly also among the most rewarding.

There was nothing mundane about those fall months I spent in tractor class, and even though at times I wondered if my desire to farm was nothing more than a crazy attempt to prove that I could adapt myself to any vocation, I got over those feelings after I became, in the eyes of the cowboys, the "expert" tractor girl. I still didn't understand how all the metal parts fit together, but no one seemed to care. And although the students were expected—as part of their grade— to fix those tractors they were driving for the day, my newfound buddies agreed to help me repair mine in exchange for sharing my special driving techniques. When my tractor would break down in the middle of a grapevine row, a couple of pals would see to it that I got on my way again. They'd jump off their own powerful vehicles and dodge through grapevine rows, crouching so our instructor wouldn't see them on their way to assist me. I laid there on my back watching them work, wondering how envious some of my old business associates would be if they knew what I was doing at that exact moment. I laughed at the idea of some of my women friends from the city seeing me here with two guys fixing my broken tractor while I lay in the middle of a breathtaking vineyard soaking up the spine-tingling California sun. When the job was done, they'd stealthily crawl on all fours so as not to be seen by the teacher, wiping their greasy hands on my shoulder as they passed by. "Fudge," I'd whisper to them, as I spit on my arm and wiped the grease away. I felt like "one of the guys."

That same fall I was also enrolled in a soil class. We mostly had lectures in the schoolroom, but sometimes we would head to the vineyards of local wineries on a school bus painted light green, the Martha Stewart green that would become popular years later. We attracted attention from police, winery workers, and pedestrians who thought our bus resembled a border-control vehicle. This caused us more than a few delays, and a few kicks for the students who were there to fill an elective slot. It meant less learning time and more entertainment. We were questioned, suspiciously stared at, and casually detained, giving us a taste of what convicts might feel like riding in a prison bus on their way to work the fields.

The driver of our bus was the infamous Professor Richard Thomas. The well-loved Sonoma County native, who has taught viticulture to thousands of farming students and whose license plate reads DR VINE, is a supremely knowledgeable viticulturist and brilliant guy who cracks spicy jokes and has a heart of gold. It's estimated that nearly seventy percent of the vineyards in Sonoma County have been planted by former Thomas students. He took his job very seriously, making sure that the viticulture students realized the impact their farming mistakes would have on our society. And his tests were brutal, requiring knowledge of every word he said during class verbatim, jokes included, to ensure the serious students wouldn't miss any of his class time.

Thomas had this advice about life: "If it's not fun, don't do it." And it's made more and more sense to me as the years have gone on. With his philosophy as our biggest motivation in tow, we usually took a mid-day break surrounded by food and wine that we'd gathered from the Sonoma County winery where we'd been working. Wineries like Dry Creek Vineyards with their Loire-like quality of Sauvignon Blanc, Geyser Peak with their impressive red blends, Sonoma Cutrer with their delicately elegant Chardonnays, and White Oak with their expert winemaking principles, all welcomed the farming students to their different regions in the county—educating, encouraging, and entertaining.

Locals were gracious with their goods and I became educated about the virtues of farm fresh produce. I interacted with savvy farmers who know the goodness of a hot sandwich warmed by the sun. Fresh from the rich earth came tomatoes, red peppers, onions, spinach, and fragrant herbs like basil, thyme, and rosemary, dropped at our feet along with warm French bread and fresh cheese. The bread came from the local baker, the cheese from the milk of the goat hanging out in the barn next to the vineyard where we worked. We'd stuff every element we could into our bread, grab a wine glass and fill it directly from a barrel in the wineries' cellars, and flop down on the ground to feast away and recap the earlier part of our day. This is where I learned to love the simplicity of food that is still warm from the ground, and of wine that skips the bottle and goes straight from the barrel to the stomach.

Professor Thomas impressed me from the first day of class when he said, "Fall is the perfect time to get started with soil. Remember that soil is in the field and dirt is on your clothes. To confuse the two is to misconstrue the essence of farming. Childhood recollections of adult voices murmuring words such as, 'Wash the dirt off your hands,' or 'Stop tracking dirt into the house,' serve no useful purpose when we're discussing our farmlands that produce so much of what we eat and contribute so many benefits toward our well being. Soil is your dearest friend and should be cherished, respected, and admired for what it allows any plant grower to produce."

I'd never really thought about soil that way. During the course of that class I not only learned to view soil as a necessary and positive resource for maintaining the health and stability of the things being grown in it, but I learned about the importance of all the living things hidden within the ground. To farm successfully I needed to promote the growth and health of all the things living in the soil. I had always looked upon them as separate entities, but the soil and its inhabitants must coexist in order for both to remain healthy. The relationship of grapevine to soil is like that of painter to paintbrush. The animation and soul of the painting can't exist without the synergistic juxtaposition of artist to tool, and the energy and vitality of the grapevine can't endure without side-by-side organism action of soil and its inhabitants.

Professor Thomas also emphasized that throughout history wild grapevines have grown and thrived. Soils that were completely untouched and left to produce whatever could survive have long been shown to produce grapevines. When soil contains an acceptable balance of sand, silt, and clay, chances are good that the grapevines will grow and produce fabulous, flavorful wine grapes. The grapevine roots can survive when deep in the ground or close to the surface; they will grow until they find what they need.

I continue to be inspired by the remarkable qualities of healthy soil, but over the course of Professor Thomas's class my exuberance was heightened. His enthusiasm and knowledge were contagious and I drove my family crazy trying to share the bits of information I had learned. At one point during the viticulture learning process, a memory that still grates on their nerves, I grabbed my three kids and brought them out to the vineyard.

"Look at that beautiful soil," I screeched. "Touch it. I want you to feel the texture and structure and tell me what you think."

"Icky, Mama," Joy said, in her two-year-old baby talk dialect.

"Wrong," I said teasingly.

Grace rolled her eyes and fidgeted saying, "The dirt is on my dress, Mom, and my sneakers, too. Get it off!"

"Not dirt, honey," I exclaimed. "Soil. My professor always says dirt is on your clothes and soil is in the ground. To confuse the two is to misinterpret a main point about farming." This was probably way too complicated for her to understand at age six, but it felt good to say it anyway.

Dude at least acted like he was interested with the hike I'd taken them on, or maybe he was just happy to be given carte blanche to roll around on the ground. Whatever it was, he could explain the differences, even if the terms he used were a bit different from the ones I'd learned in class. "Yeah, Mom, dirt is nasty and sticky, and soil is good and soft." Oh well, I told myself, they'll understand some day.

When my exuberance about soils surged, I found that my entire outlook on farming changed. I was no longer wary, but respectful. I understood that to farm was not my right, but a privilege—a privilege that should be learned. And I also understood why farmers actually use tractors. They are a way to create and introduce new life into the soil, a way to make the soil come alive by breaking down the solid matter and churning up the billions of microorganisms that are needed to further decompose the nutrients and make them more available to crops. Without healthy alive soil the grapevines will not produce fruit. I also learned that while driving a tractor one must concentrate on changing gears, braking, and turning, and that the giant machine takes precedence over everything. Most of all, the loud clanging noise of the engine becomes therapeutic, blocking out the clatter from the tireless echo of our brains.

HOW TO DETERMINE THE SOIL THAT'S BEST FOR YOUR GARDEN

1. Call the Natural Resource Conservation Service, a federal agency with offices nationwide. They offer preprinted soil surveys for many locations throughout the United States, and include data on soil type, permeability, texture, and mineral content.

2. Do a visual and tactile soil test of your own. Dig a hole and inspect the soil texture, looking for silt, which will be slick and slippery and resemble kernels of corn; sand, which will be gritty and not unlike sand at the beach; and clay, which will be very sticky and thick.

3. Do the "mayonnaise test" that I learned in viticulture school: Take an empty mayonnaise jar, fill it with one cup of dirt—oops, soil—then fill it with water to the top of the jar. Add three tablespoons of powdered dishwasher soap and shake the jar for five minutes. After the jar has stood for 40 seconds, there will be a layer of sand; after 40 minutes a layer of silt; and after 24 hours a layer of clay.

4. Drive to your local gardening store. Ask for assistance and buy a bag of planting soil (whatever size is needed for the planting pot that you have selected for your grapevine).

✳ ✳ ✳

Once you know the ratio of silt, sand, and clay in your soil, you will know how to manage the vines you grow in it. The best soil is a good loam consisting of about 35% silt, 45% sand, and 20% clay, which drains well and causes the least amount of nutrient leaching. Soil with a high sand content causes water to drain rapidly through its large pores, carrying with it nutrients your vines will need. Soil with a high clay content will retain water, drain poorly, and result in nutrient lumping.

In choosing the actual site for planting or placing your vines, look for areas with good sun exposure, no large trees with lots of roots to compete for nutrients and good air flow, and not too windy or likely to expose the grapes to harsh weather. If you can't find a flat or gradually sloped area, pick an old, dilapidated fence, an arbor, or even an eave up the sunny side of your house. As my astute mother always says about raising children, "They will survive in spite of you and despite you."

Take heed of Professor Thomas's tip that grapevines can grow in many different types of earth—small areas (pots) or large areas (farmlands) and under many adverse conditions (including the adversity of an ignorant grower). A grapevine has feeder roots that extend underground to a depth determined by the texture and structure of the soil. If you acquire a basic knowledge of your soil, you will know most of what you'll need to know to manage the grapevines within your own specific situation.

One of my favorite places to take people to show them how adaptable grapevines are is at the Benziger Family Winery in Glen Ellen, California. Situated in the middle of acres of vineyard, rolling hills, and a very successful winery, is one lone grapevine planted in a clear plastic pot. The pot is about two-feet wide by about six-feet deep, and any touring wine country spectator can view exactly what is occurring with the roots of the plant. It's a fabulous way to see what your vine will look like underground, and also a great way to view different layers of soil, rocks, and the other stuff to which the grapevine adapts. Most of all, it exposes how unbelievably pliant grapevines really are.

TWO

THE FUTURE BELONGS TO THOSE WHO BELIEVE IN THEIR VINE

*I*n my early days of learning to farm, there were problems. Chuck was blowing his way through nineteen-hour days, seven days a week. I couldn't count on him for anything. The house had a huge repertoire of voices that didn't bother me during the day but at nighttime brought all the demons of my childhood racing back into my mind. Loud noises resembling human footsteps and jarrings and rockings from all parts of the two-story stucco dwelling aroused my terror and my protective instincts simultaneously. Country nights are unbelievably dark when you're used to city "dark," and because my husband was not home most evenings, and my three children lay soundly sleeping, I felt fears I hadn't felt in decades. Our nearest neighbors were remote by my city standards, and I thought about how I would protect Grace, Dude, and Joy if an intruder actually came on my property. The locals tried to tell me that these were just fears and that the reality of those fears were unfounded, but I still wrestled with feelings of inadequacy.

"This is farming country," they said, "you'd best be concerned with growing quality grapes that can produce good wine, and learning how to take care of your land." But my concerns about our isolation continued and they made me wonder if we had made the wrong choice about taking our children away from the city. Much of my reasoning behind a move to the country was that it would be safer for the kids, free from the dangers of the city, free from the drugs of urban living, and free from the toxicity of growing up without nature close at hand. The helplessness was stemming from unfamiliarity and the loneliness of those nights when my husband wasn't home.

The creakings and rumblings of my home produced great insight into the soil where my dwelling was situated, and the soil where my grapevines were growing. It forced me to ask questions about my soil that I wouldn't have otherwise thought about, which ultimately led me to adapt my growing practices so as to produce a more perfect soil. What could I do to amend my soil so that it resembled a "perfect" loam soil—soil with the perfect mixture of silt, sand, and clay? Soil that drained well and leached the least amount of nutrients? Soil that made the healthiest environment for the grapevines?

On my twenty-four acres of clay soil, I needed to devote my best energy to finding out how to improve my soil structure (unless I wanted to start a pottery company). Viticulture classes had only proffered me one solution for boosting soil health: synthetic fertilizers. I had questions about the environmental impact and overall long-term effect of this type of fertilizing. (I knew that my vineyard was around ten years old and had been farmed using synthetic fertilizers and chemical sprays.) What alternatives could I explore that would improve the health of my land and its ecosystem?

My three big questions became:
1. Do I want to amend my soil with natural compost and mulch?
2. Do I want to amend my soil with synthetic fertilizers?
3. Do I want to leave my soil alone, watch my vines, and then make a decision based on the health of the vine?

The creakings and rumblings of my home also initiated another much bigger problem. A few times that first fall I went so far as to call the police, who probably thought I could use a dose of therapy to ease my concerns. But on many of those terror-ridden nights, panic surfaced sooner than logic and my trembling fingers had dialed my local police station before I'd talked myself into calming down. As I waited those long minutes that seemed like hours, I would circle around the rooms of my children wildly looking in all directions like an expectant coyote ready to pounce its unseen prey. When I felt like I could handle any trespasser—my adrenaline flowing, ready to protect my children from any unsightly overstepper who would dare pass beyond my threshold—I'd redial the police station ready to make a convincing confession stating that there wasn't a problem at all and that it was just the wind whistling through the chimneys and the rain smashing against my eaves.

"Oh no, Mrs. Moulton," the dispatcher would say, "he's already on his way." I'd patter downstairs in my bare feet and disheveled lacy night attire, wishing to be anyone else at that precise moment, and sure enough there'd be the police car's bright stream of lights issuing down the dark, country road.

The cop who came in response to my calls spoke calmly about the "safeness" of where I lived and spouted the local crime statistics. I knew right away that a lecture was coming when the policeman sat me down on the stairs, my teeth chattering and feet shaking, and stood looking down at me as if I were a child caught thieving from the neighbor's house. My cold hands clutched the ruffles at the neck of my nightgown; I guess I thought I was protecting my vulnerable heart. Jokingly, he said, "Look, princess, maybe you should look for a full-time man who could comfort you at night."

"Excuse me," I snapped, "I have a husband; it's just that he works very long hours."

"Oh, I see. Well, get a watchdog then."

Whether it was to spite that condescending cop, or whether I was simply adjusting to living in relative wilderness, things did get better. When I told Chuck about the police visit he agreed with the cop about getting a dog, "Why don't we get one of those mastiff dogs that are supposed to be so territorial and protective?"

Sha-na-na was the name given to our 110-pound mastiff puppy, named by the breeder after her son's favorite television character. She was protective all right; so protective she wouldn't even let

Chuck near me. Sha-na-na brought with her all the troubles puppies normally do. Dinnertime required stamina, both strength of body and fortitude of mind, as she slobbered and chowed down her meals at our feet. Her fully masticated dinner would fly in all directions around my kitchen. Either she did not like my cooking or I was very naïve about her big-dog eating habits, but Dude loved it since finally there was someone in the house that made more mess than he did.

"Mom, just feed her outside," Dude said after a feeding got especially messy and I got particularly annoyed with the dog.

One of her biggest faults was that she insisted on monopolizing the couch most of the day, and there was absolutely no way to get her off. Since she took up the entire space, and I couldn't budge her by tugging on her collar, I'd have to attach her leash, brace myself against the adjacent wall, and swiftly yank with all my strength. She'd reluctantly slither to the floor and with great speed we'd all jump on the free space before she could lumber her way back to her cushy spot.

I did have comforting visions of Sha-na-na attacking any and all unwanted guests, human or otherwise, that may have decided to venture onto my property during the day or night. I soon found this to be shortsighted, however, when, on her second evening with us, she stood at the door (for nearly three hours) howling to be let out. I tried everything to divert her attention from the doorway; but have you ever tried to negotiate with a slobbering 110-pound puppy? It's kind of like dealing with a stubborn teenager. My front-door diversions—biscuits, toys, and even a shoe—didn't work and the wailing continued until I finally opened the door and let her out. Big mistake. After two hours of listening to her run around the property, barking at anything that remotely resembled a threat, I nearly went crazy. The barking, however bad it was, didn't compare—at least for me—with the embarrassment of ten phone calls and nasty threats I received from a distant neighbor.

I grabbed my coat and wandered around the property in the dark looking for her. When I finally caught her, it wasn't a pretty picture. She didn't respond to food (her dinner was still on my wall) so I had to get close enough to throw a bucket of water on her, startle her, and then throw a towel over her head. I knew this would work because I'd used it years ago on my stubborn black standard poodle. Although this sounds very inhumane, the alternatives were far crueler, believe me. Once I got the towel over her head I swung a noosed rope around her neck and began to tug, pulling her in the direction of the house. I've never had any experience lassoing horses or cattle, and I'm nearly certain that rodeo performers don't begin by pouring buckets of water over the animal's head and tossing delicate bathroom towels over their eyes; nonetheless, I think my technique was clever and may have earned me some high marks with most rodeo audiences. But Sha-na-na was one stubborn animal—even more than the poodle—and we looked pretty silly, each of us pulling our hardest in opposite directions.

On my way back to the house in complete darkness with Sha-na-na lumbering behind, I fell into a ditch. My ankle snapped in three places and I lay at the bottom of a giant hole. I've never known fear the way I knew it at that moment. "Doggonnit," I yelped. I could smell every detail of the damp soil. I'd never smelled the earth that way before; it was as if my senses had been previously dead and just awakened. But I was alone—completely alone—and it was a strange

44

feeling. It seemed like an eternity by the time I managed to crawl back to the house, and before I was able to call Chuck at his office.

I was emotionally wounded by the accident. Chuck says my father drove Sha-na-na back to her original home. I have no recollection of it. I only remember that I had an itchy full-length cast and uncomfortable crutches, that I couldn't move much for two months, that my house was disorderly, and that I couldn't take care of Grace, Dude, and Joy—or the land.

Not long after my accident, Chuck told me how pleased he was with our decision to move to the country.

"You are?" I asked. "Even though I've completely botched up my end of the deal?" My ankle was still healing and I was not much help on the land.

"Definitely," he said, "this is just a minor glitch for you."

"You're right," I assured myself, thinking about one of my favorite old sayings, *the future belongs to those who believe in the beauty of their dreams.* I just needed to forget about my short-term problem and focus on the bigger picture. Still, the short-term problem needed to be solved.

"Can't you just come home and take care of me?" I begged Chuck. "You're my husband." But Chuck was still running his doctor race. That solution wouldn't work.

✳ ✳ ✳

Rachel, an English girl with a take-charge attitude who had won a special award in England for arresting a violent street criminal by manipulating him into a confession, was the best thing that could have happened to me. A Birmingham, England, police officer-in-training, she'd responded to a call from a corner grocery store clerk who'd been robbed and taken at knifepoint. She chased and caught the shoplifter and successfully calmed him down long enough to ask him if she could bum a fag. He pulled out the stolen cigarettes and the weapon as well. Rachel was a hero; she was given an award, a promotion, and high praise for "using polite words to cajole a guilty, violent criminal." Beyond being resourceful with her words, she was a savior during a time when I really needed someone around. My kids adored her from the moment she entered our house, and she was extremely hard working when it came to tending the vines. She was in her twenties when she arrived in the States, having come to get away from the streets of Birmingham for a year and study about life in the California wine country.

She had only been in the States for a short period when Chuck found her agency's ad in our local newspaper. He telephoned them, without my knowing, and expressed an interest in having one of their clients live in our home. We got matched up with Rachel because she was interested in living in the country, and because I was interested in having a trained policewoman at my beck and call. It was to be the perfect match: the female quasi-farmer or farmer-in-training meets the English woman police officer-in-training.

"Should I serve her Sauvignon Blanc, Viognier, or Chardonnay when she arrives?" I asked Chuck, when he surprised me with the news that I would be having an English girl helping me around the farm for a while until my leg was better. "Because I'm thinking it would be friendly to welcome her with some wine from our region the minute she arrives in Glen Ellen. I think a crisp, cool, slightly sweet white wine would be best because it's fall and still so hot. I thought a nice Viognier from Glen Ellen Winery with its exotic, floral flavor might be nice." She was arriving mid-day. I was determined to be hospitable and make her feel at home.

"Don't get all worked up about it," Chuck said. "Just serve her tea. The English love tea."

In the end I served her a lovely Sauvignon Blanc from Benziger Winery, a local winery next door to me (as the crow flies). The wine was inviting, harmonious, and soothingly sweet. It was the perfect compliment to the chatty, warm conversation we had.

A couple of days after Rachel arrived, I fell down the stairs. My crutches ended up flying in all directions and my casted leg banged hard against the wooden steps.

"Shasta!" I cried under my breath. I was trying to sneak out of the house and visit the vineyard and my vegetable garden. Rachel came running when she heard the commotion.

"What exactly are you doing?" she questioned in her pleasant British accent. "You're supposed to be in bed, remember?"

"I know," I said, "but I'm missing the rich smell of the sun-ripened tomatoes, their sweet taste powdered with musty earth, and I'm missing the harmonious whiffs of star jasmine on my way to the vegetable garden."

"You're missing a tomato?" Rachel said, perplexed by what she thought was an inane reason. This was an easy answer, though she couldn't have imagined the way I missed the smell of my tomatoes, and all the other smells I was missing from my upstairs bedroom, but I was missing outside time with my kids even more.

So I took the easy route. "Yes," I lied, thinking of the stinging hot days with my kids hanging out in our vegetable garden. I had a perfect memory of picking vegetables while Grace, in just her bathing suit and red suede cowboy boots, watered the dry soil; Dude, wearing his suede jodhpurs with lasso in hand roped lizards; and Joy squeezed a strawberry in each fist until the sweet juice spurted out and dribbled its way down her arm. I missed what happened after the picking when I'd headed up to the house to caramelize the red onions and roast the red peppers for homemade vegetable and goat cheese pizza. I missed the time when we'd sat down to a civilized meal of thickly sliced beefsteak tomatoes with a slab of buffalo mozzarella and fresh basil topped with local olive oil and balsamic vinegar, accompanied by our steaming hot pizza. That type of day and meal had become our favorite pastime of the fall season. That was what I really wanted and couldn't have.

That night, because I didn't want Chuck to know that I'd fallen down the stairs, and because I wanted to see and feel my leg, Rachel and I split open the cast using scissors and a screwdriver and hammer from Dude's toy carpenter set. The swelling was so bad that I couldn't stand the tightness anymore.

"I just need to touch my foot," I begged Rachel, "You gotta help me get this cast open."

We taped the cast back with cloth tape that matched the cast color—almost—and Grace, Dude, and Joy drew all over it to disguise the opening. I wore sweats to cover it for the next six weeks and Chuck never knew.

At my next doctor's appointment the x-rays showed the break had healed in position, despite my carelessness. Rachel splurged on a bottle of Dom Perignon, named after a famous French monk of the mid-1600s who was considered to be the biggest influence in the development of Champagne. Remembered for his creative grape-growing and gifted winemaking, his name was adopted in the 1920s by the famous French Champagne Moet et Chandon when they decided to name their supreme Champagne after him. In that moment I could recall how at the young age of fourteen—soon after my brother's death—it felt to taste the sweet, bubbly inspiration of French Champagne when my parents took my sister and I to the region of Champagne in northeastern France to Moet et Chandon so we could recover our hope and rediscover the beauty of tradition and heritage. The night my doctor gave me the thumbs up on my healing process, Rachel and I sat in the wine cellar surrounded by the 2,000 bottles of wine Chuck and I had acquired when we bought the house. We celebrated with this famous monk's Champagne as a tribute to his aged passion of grape-growing and winemaking, to the beauty of history, and to my relief over the healed leg.

"What are you so happy about?" Chuck asked, late that night when he came home and found us sitting on the wine cellar floor drinking French Champagne and doing our nails.

"Oh, nothing," we laughed. He seemed a bit hurt that we wouldn't tell him, and that we had secrets he didn't know about.

We bonded after that bottle of champagne and Rachel ended up staying many more years, long after my leg had healed. She became mesmerized by California wine country living, just like us, and we took turns chasing the bugs away from the grapevines, pouring buckets of water on the vines that were missed by the drip lines, cleaning the farm equipment, pruning the vines, thinning the crop, riding the tractor, and everything else it took to work the land. I had the knowledge (most of the time) and Rachel had the pleasant words.

BOOSTING YOUR SOIL'S HEALTH

Composting

Compost, a natural or organic soil amendment, holds countless benefits for gardeners who want to maintain good-quality soil. The best thing about compost is that it actually helps change the soil's structure. Humeric acid, which is generated by the compost, allows the silt, sand, and clay particles to bind together to produce a more structurally sound, or loam, soil. The benefits of composting are quick, relatively inexpensive, and can be done even before you plant your grapevines and again each year after harvest.

My earliest experiences with composting occurred thirty years ago as I watched my grandfather dump the dregs of his early-morning coffee, the coffee grounds, and some eggshells directly onto his vegetable garden. I soon learned that he was an incredibly productive backyard gardener and his soils were exceptionally fertile. His apple tree, which he had experimentally grafted, produced five different types of apples.

Although my grandfather appreciated the shock value of dumping his breakfast remains into his garden, I recommend that you make sure that your organic matter is completely rotted before you put it back into the soil. When the debris is not completely decomposed, it will not contain sufficient bacteria and the compost will draw nitrogen from the soil, causing a nitrogen deficiency in the vines.

The main thing to remember is that compost consists of three basic elements: 1) soil, usually from plant roots that are high in microbes and break down the other materials into compost; 2) carbon, which comes from paper, wood chips, dried leaves, and dried flowers; and 3) nitrogen, produced from kitchen scraps, weeds, and grass clippings. It will not take much garden space if you put these remnants into a wooden composting bin, and after six months to a year the compost should be ready. All you need to do is give a few stirs throughout the process in order to keep the bacteria thriving and continue the rotting process. Another way to make compost would be to mix 30% yard clippings, 40% pomace (from the wine you make), and 30% chicken, turkey, horse, sheep, pig, or cow manure. Or, if you prefer, you can buy compost from local waste management or private companies. Not only will compost improve your soil's overall texture and structure, it can also:

- improve soil drainage and water-retention capabilities,
- improve aeration by adding organic matter,
- provide a slow release of nutrients and trace elements to soil,
- add beneficial microorganisms that help break down nutrients,
- help to warm the soil by absorbing the sun's rays.

Thus, for clay soils, composting helps provide better drainage and oxygen availability, and for sandy soils it can help provide better water-retention capabilities.

Purchasing an acid/alkaline (pH) test kit from your local nursery may be a good idea. Composting may change the pH of the soil and if you begin with this test you can insure that the levels remain acceptable. The optimal pH level for grapevines is between 6.0 and 6.5, but levels anywhere from 5.5 to 7.0 are still acceptable. If the level is 7.5 or above, the soil will be less acidic; if the soil is 5.8 or below, the soil will be more acidic. In general, soils that are less acidic, or more alkaline, prevail in areas with little rainfall, and more acidic soils are common to areas with heavier rainfall.

The pH levels in the soil can be changed by:

- adding wood ash or lime to make an acid soil more alkaline,
- adding pine needles, coffee grounds, or elemental sulfur to make an alkaline soil more acidic,
- adding compost to neutralize both acid and alkaline soils.

Synthetic Fertilizers

A second option is to treat your soil with commercially produced fertilizers. There are many different forms of both dry and liquid synthesized fertilizers, with varying amounts of nitrogen, phosphorous, and potassium (NPK). Ensuring the correct combination of fertilizer is tricky, and you'll need to perform a soil analysis (every couple of years) to establish nutrient levels.

Local gardening stores sell soil test kits that can be used to test the NPK of the soil. Or hire a professional soil analysis laboratory to analyze the mineral content, and proceed with treating the soil based on its specific deficiencies.

Gamble

The third option, after composting and synthetic fertilizing, is to leave the soil alone and see what happens with your vines. Gamblers have personalities that glory in risk-taking. I am not a gambler; doing nothing would cause the farmer in me unacceptably high levels of anxiety and frustration. Remember, though, grapevines can survive many abuses, and the wait-and-see approach might work well for you as a backyard gardener growing grapes on a small-scale basis.

Regardless of whether you compost, synthetically fertilize, or do nothing at all, soil depth also plays a role in how your grapevines respond. In shallow soil, vines produce a smaller crop and need more frequent irrigation, whereas in a deeper, fertile soil they produce heavier crops with less irrigation. Soil depth relates to water drainage within the soil. In other words, a solid layer of rock or compacted soil that forms a barrier will not allow the roots to penetrate, nor will water be able to drain. If they need to, grapevines can extend their roots more than 10 feet and produce large amounts of grapes because of their fertile depths. They can grow in 18 inches of soil or 18 feet of soil.

RULE: The deeper the soil, free of any obstruction or hardpan, the deeper will be the roots and the more productive the vine.

THREE

THE GRAPE DOESN'T FALL TOO FAR FROM THE VINE

*A*fter a couple of seasons of farming grapes in Glen Ellen, Chuck and I decided to take a trip to the south of Italy to study Italian vineyards and drink some Italian wine—a business trip of sorts. Rachel took care of the kids while we were gone. The trip turned out to be one of the most eye-opening experiences of my life; instead of traipsing through large wineries touring vineyard land with busloads of people, as occurs in California, we found no giant estates with acres and acres of vineyards, and no Disneyland-type trams leading up to luxurious tasting rooms. It seemed that each individual household grew a few of their own vines, from which they made their own wine purely for their own enjoyment and consumption.

Perched on the edge of the Amalfi Coast with binoculars dangling from my neck, I gazed endlessly at Italian home vineyard

styles, taking mental notes and soaking it all in. Small houses speck-
led the cliffs; primitive arbors made from irregular pieces of wood
and sticks were tied together haphazardly with old rope. Red roofs,
yellow doors, pink window frames, and old rock walls bathed the
entire mélange of landscape. But the most dramatic and compelling
aspect of the scenery was the grapevines, found in places where one
might expect to see ugly weeds, their wild arms climbing through
every crevice of every arbor, cascading over tables, chairs, and even
garbage cans, making everything look alive with their vibrant
energy. The technique was both practical and rustic.

It was true that the grapevines sprawled over the arbors provided a primitive and useful shading system for the small homes,
but there was something of a much more provocative elegance. The
style and beauty of the flowing limbs elicited a bucolic, countrified
feeling, even though we were in a crowded city. I was touched by the
growers' clever use of small spaces and how adaptable the grapevines
were to areas no bigger than a tiny balcony. Some of the vines were
even growing out of clay pots and yet they evoked the feeling of an
expansive tropical paradise. It was a most amazing collage of Mother
Nature, brilliantly created with limited space and the simplicity of
grapevines. And it was there for everyone—not just farmers and
those with large pieces of land. The stimulating grace of the grapevines and the manner in which the Italians captured this beauty was
inspiring.

The Italians made use of their limited space by growing lemon
trees on the ground and then training grapevines to grow ten feet
or so up over the top of the tree. What a funny sight it was: lemon
trees bearing fruit with super-tall grapevines hanging over them like

some sort of wacky paradise from a Dr. Seuss children's book. Sometimes black netting was spread over the treetops, making it look as if the grapevines were sprouting from the nets themselves. These intricate "trellises" grew on plots of land no more than five- by ten-feet and they dotted the cliffs of the stunning coastline facing in all directions. The Amalfi home-growers' innovative gardening practices made use of every inch of space; they wasted nothing.

✳ ✳ ✳

I returned to my northern California farm with the Italian experience firmly lodged in the forefront of my mind—with ideas for spreading some of these newfound systems. I could think of nothing else.

"Why couldn't Americans, and people from other countries, no matter how limited their space, follow in the footsteps of the Italians and create their own mini-vineyards and wineries?" I asked Rachel, as we sat around talking about my trip. I already knew that grapes were being grown in forty-nine states in the United States, and not even in specific grape-growing regions.

"Hey, Rach," I said, as I dragged my suitcase up and over the wooden steps leading to my room. "I bet you could even grow grapes in your backyard in England—if the protocol was right."

"You're crazy," she said.

"Nope, I bet you could do it, and only a step away from the doorstep of your charming English brownstone, in a sunny spot on your balcony or porch, or on the eaves of your roof or fence pickets, or within the brightest nook or corner of your backyard. You

EXACTLY HOW MANY GRAPEVINES DO YOU NEED TO PRODUCE A BOTTLE OF WINE?

Assume that each grapevine (after a couple years of growth, depending on your growing practices) will produce anywhere from 8 to 12 pounds of grapes. It takes roughly 16 pounds of fruit (if you don't lose a lot of juice between your toes while stomping or drink too much after pressing) to produce one gallon of wine. Conservatively, if you figure that each vine will get 8 pounds of fruit, then 20 grapevines will give you approximately 50 bottles of wine. Grapevines will cost anywhere from $3.00 to $7.00 apiece, depending upon where you live, the variety of plant, and the quantity purchased. When you think about it, the Italians are smart to set up shop in their own backyards.

know—where you have weeds growing now." We were making our way toward the kitchen now.

Rachel, in her extremely practical way, wasn't quite sure. "I don't know," she mused, "you always make things look so easy. And it might be hard to find a sunny spot with English climate."

"I've got an answer for that," I said. "You can add sugar to the must when you make wine. Here's what I think," I continued, watching Rachel and Joy prepare fresh guacamole (Joy squeezing the avocado until green slime covered her fingers) with sliced red onions, jalapeño peppers, tomatoes, and fresh lime juice. "In the same way people think nothing of planting strawberries and making strawberry jam, they could plant grapevines and make a little wine. The Italians do it. I'm not saying that a suburban or city gardener will ever compete with commercial grape-growers or famous winemakers of the world, but I think that the beauty, inspiration, and creative energies of this industry could be more widely shared and partially reproduced."

"Paula, I don't know," she said skeptically. We sat back and dipped our baked corn tortillas into the fresh guacamole and drank Chardonnay from the Kunde Winery, located no more than a few miles away from our property.

"Yes, yes, yes," I replied. "With a few simple tools and the know-how to make it happen, the next bottle of wine you bring to a party could be wine from your own mini-vineyard. What do you say, Rach?"

Chuck left for work and I blathered on about how I thought others should be able to experience the beauty and fun of grape-growing and winemaking—not just farmers and winery owners. I remembered professor Thomas saying how incredibly hearty grapevines are and how easily they can adapt to their environment. "Each grapevine is a self-sufficient growing unit capable of vegetative growth, life, and fruit production. A vine consists of many parts, such as root systems, shoots, leaves, trunk, and flowers, which eventually produce the grape clusters; and each of these parts has a prominent function necessary for the overall health and productive life of the vine."

VINE ANATOMY

I think grapevines are similar to the human body and envision the vine with three major parts, each corresponding to parts of the human body: the roots of the vine to our feet; the trunk to our torso; the shoots to our head.

Feet

The roots of a grapevine function as its anchors to the earth. From this anchorage the vine receives the water and minerals it needs to survive by its roots' contact with the soil. Our feet, for most of us, are the support for our bodies; they are stability, security, and sustenance for our frame. In comparing our feet to the root of the vine, I decided that if I remembered two key elements that pertain to feet—anchor and sustenance—then I would never forget the function of grapevine roots.

Torso

The trunk of the vine provides the pathway on which the nutrients that the roots absorb from the soil move up to the aboveground parts of the vine. At full maturity the trunk of the vine stops growing and grows only in width. The trunk is thus a physical support system for the vine as well as a storage chamber. Just like grapevines, our torsos are part of our support system. They are our storage chamber for food and, unfortunately, as with grapevines, they usually get wider once we stop growing taller.

Head

The shoots are the third major structural component of a vine. Shoots are more complex in their function because in addition to providing stability for the fruit, they are the parts of the vine that actually produce the crop. Shoots grow from buds on the vine. New shoots are green and become brown canes after they drop their leaves in the fall. As the years progress the new canes turn from thin brown smooth wood to thick rough peely wood, and it is safe to assume that the thicker the diameter of the wood the older the cane. A grower needs to understand all the parts of the shoot if she is to keep her vines healthy and productive.

Along the shoots are slight bumps called nodes. The leaves develop on alternate sides of these nodes. Each node will produce a bud. The flower clusters, which eventually turn into berry clusters, grow in the first to sixth node range. At the joint, where each leaf attaches to the shoot, is a bud. Each bud will carry within its unit an active and a dormant bud. The active bud will grow the year it develops with a single growing point, and can also produce another growth called a "lateral." The laterals look like shoots but are smaller and younger. The laterals can produce a second crop, but it is considered undesirable to let this occur since it overly stresses the vine.

The dormant bud will only grow in its second year and will be responsible for the shoots and crop for the next season. Located in the dormant bud will be its primary, secondary, and tertiary parts, which together make up an ingenious system of protection for the grapevine. If Mother Nature produces an early frost and wipes out the primary bud, there is a secondary bud waiting in line to produce the crop. In reality, that single bud holds the key to the production of shoots, leaves, flower clusters, and eventually the fruit of the grapevine.

Green shoots that have turned into brown canes, after harvest and before pruning, look like a head with a giant mass of wild hair flying in all directions (from a distance, that is).

"It isn't really all that complicated if you just understand how grapevines actually grow," I continued.

As I turned around to see if anyone was listening I saw Grace, Dude, Joy, and Rachel standing at the window looking out toward the vineyard. Grace invited me to come look. She was around eight at the time.

"Moo moo," Joy laughed. I walked over to the window to see what was so exciting, thinking one of the kids had painted a cow banner in honor of my return home from Italy.

"Shasta! There's a brown cow out there," I shouted. (We didn't have cows; only vineyards and our twenty-four acres were deer-fenced.)

Rachel just looked at me. She was so responsible and so level headed. I could see that she hadn't known what to do about the cow.

I didn't want to make her feel bad by asking a bunch of questions like *did you call anyone for help?* or *did you try and get him off the property?* She assured me that she'd been watching the grapes and they were fine.

"I thought we'd deal with it together when you got home," she said. We handled everything around the farm this way.

The cow kept appearing at odd places around the exterior of our home. We became interested in this curious animal with its soft-looking warm face and spunky personality. In fact, we became so attached that we wanted to name the animal. The problem was that we couldn't choose a name unless we knew the sex. This inevitably led to long discussions, and sometimes arguments, about the sex of the animal. How many semi-intelligent people does it actually take to determine the sex of a bovine? If you're in my family, it took all six of us—two American parents, one English adult, and three American children. That darn steer was so fast that every time we got close enough to look underneath the torso, it would run off at such great speed that none of us could determine whether that thing hanging down was a male part or a female part. The cow was fast and we were slow. Days were filled with endless argument about the genitalia of that cuddly looking animal. It was finally determined that it was a castrated male, which would mean it was a steer.

When I called Fish and Game and then Animal Control, five days after the steer had arrived, they were shocked that it had taken me so long to call them about the missing animal. "He's fast, really fast," I said.

"I'm not sure what you mean by 'he's fast,' Miss," said a confused Animal Control official on the other end of the line.

"Oh, nothing," I replied. I sure as heck wasn't going to tell him that we couldn't let the steer go until we had determined the sex, our own little family obsession. He wouldn't understand the oddities of my family. This had turned into a race, a battle of the sexes if you will, and we were not going to let go until one side or the other had won the contest—female or male, which was it?

We were all becoming very attached to the steer; he was a part of the family now. I had even spent the previous evening driving around in the dark looking for him. My father, involved via telephone, warned me about the heaviness of a dead steer. "What do you mean the heaviness of a dead steer?" I said.

"Well, have you given it any food or water?" my dad asked.

Things never change. My dad had always been the one to ask that question when we were growing up. He had never been the one to feed or water our animals (we did that), but he was certainly the one most concerned with whether they were properly taken care of. And his fetishes about food and water didn't stop with the family pets; they also seeped into the way he overfed and overwatered his plants. There was no conserving for him when it came to these issues.

Amazingly, I had completely forgotten about supplying food and water in our quest to determine the animal's sex. "Jeez, I forgot, Dad. There's plenty for him to eat around here, but there isn't any water." I panicked, jumped in my car—despite the blackness of the night—and drove all over my property looking for the steer. Where was he when I needed him? (He was male all right, and I was on the team who had determined this.) I couldn't find him, but I left buckets of fresh water at various places on the property.

The next morning as Chuck was on his way to work, he nearly hit the steer who was happily standing in the middle of our road, swinging his tail and batting his long eyelashes—very much alive. He called later that day to tell me that he wanted to keep the steer. "No, honey, we can't just keep him. He's not ours," I said.

"I know, but I've grown attached to him," he said.

I couldn't believe it. "What do you mean, *you've* grown attached to him?" I exclaimed. "I'm the one whose been following him around for five days, the one who carried buckets of water across my shoulders like a woman walking the dirt roads of China. And besides, he's not ours to keep."

As I was explaining the events of the previous evening to my mother, about the ruts my car nearly got stuck in, and about the stench in the back of my car from spilled buckets of water that had left a rancid-smelling odor, I could hear her carrying on a two-way conversation—one with me and one with my father. "Kenneth, did you tell your daughter that animal needed water immediately or he would die?" she snapped. Water had been an ongoing source of family disturbance and an endless argument between my parents ever since the droughts in Northern California. My mother wanted to conserve water no matter what the ramifications were: dead plants, smelly children, thirsty animals; but my father wholeheartedly disagreed and would sneak around late at night spraying the plants with extra water and filling the pets' bowls with fresh water (even if there was still water left over from the morning feedings). They had always had conflicting beliefs when it came to water. I could hear my father in the background puttering around in the kitchen. "Yes, Karol, I did." I yelled for my father's benefit because this time I was glad I'd listened to his prodigious question, "Dad, you were right, the cow was thirsty, but he's doing well now. Thanks for your suggestion."

* * *

Animal Control suggested that we call around to our neighbors and see if anyone had lost a steer (ingenious plan) and it turned out that one of the neighbors above us on Sonoma Mountain knew whose animal it was. The owner was ecstatic to find her seven-month-old steer. His young age explained the cuteness of his face and the softness of his hair. I was delighted to finally have it confirmed that the animal was indeed male, and that the girls on this farm had decisively won the sex debate.

The owner came the next morning, very early, and by the time I'd returned from dropping the kids off at school, she was still chasing the steer. It took many hours and while I was working I spied them, the owner and her two dogs, chasing the animal back and forth across our property. "I think he likes it here," she yelled at me while I was checking the grapevines, "and by the way, he looks healthier than he looked a week ago."

"He must have found water somewhere," I said.

"Yep, and he made a little bed for himself up by your water tank." His healthiness suddenly made sense. "He must be smarter than I thought," she said.

She couldn't catch him, though, and after many hours she finally went back to her own property to retrieve a mother cow. The surrogate mother was successful at calling him and the owner was able to get close enough to lasso him and take him back to the herd. She called me that night and said he was doing fine, apologizing profusely for his disobedience. "We enjoyed him and learned from him," I said. "He can come back anytime." (I left out the details of our sex-determination contest.) But we became so attached to that cute cow that in honor of his presence the bucket of water still stands in the field where we first found him.

* * *

After the cow left, I read an article in the local newspaper titled "Flavor vs. Fertilizer." The story was about French winemaker Nicolas Joly, a famous white wine maker in France. He said, "Every winegrower should have at least one cow in his house. You can learn so much from your cow." I'd hoped he didn't mean "literally" in the house. But as I read on, I found out that he believes cows and other animals can provide valuable nutrients to the soil, simply because their excrement acts as a fertilizer for the soil. It's the natural, ecological way to grow grapes. He claims that his grapes are grown with a herd of cattle—for their nitrogen-enriched manure— and a pasture full of horses to cultivate the manure into the soil. Cows are soulful, and this he believes, might actually make his wine more calming and soothing. Our steer had discovered that the grass was greener and more tasty on our land, and in the process I had discovered that the cow was beneficial to my grapevines. Our cow introduction would turn out to be a sign of what was to come.

FOUR

THE VINE IS IN THE EYE
OF THE GROWER

*T*hree years into our country living adventure I started to become troubled by the unhealthiness of my vines. Their crop load was diminishing and their growth had declined. The wineries I'd contracted to sell my fruit to—Ravenswood and Glen Ellen—were getting anxious for more fruit, so I called in a few experts to take a look. The news was bad, and unanimous. "You've got phylloxera," they all concurred separately. Phylloxera is an aphid-like bug—invisible to the naked eye—that attacks the vine's root system, eventually taking away the nutrients that are needed to sustain the grapevine, ultimately girdling or strangling the plant. I was beside myself.

"It's not all bad. You'll get to start over," Rachel cooed, trying to console me. "It'll be fun to replant the vineyard, set up a new trellis system, and train your grapes exactly the way you want."

You're right," I sulked, "there's something to be said about doing things your own way right from the start." I wasn't sure I believed my own words. But it was certainly true that the four acres of Chardonnay, two acres of Cabernet Sauvignon, and half acre of Merlot vines I owned were already established when I bought my land, and not necessarily trained the way I would want them to be if I'd planted them myself.

The ironic thing about phylloxera is that it is native to the U.S.; grapevines that grow naturally are resistant to the pest. But in the mid-1800s, East Coast grape-growers searching for high-quality, wine-producing grapes unsuspectingly shipped infested vines to France, where they were grafted with French grapes and imported back into the United States. To a grape-grower, phylloxera is the equivalent of a horrible, incurable disease that causes nothing but grief and pain.

The information on how to deal with phylloxera was ambiguous: rip out the vines immediately and plant with resistant rootstocks, or as Professor Thomas said, "Baby the vines and they might survive." The then pioneers of farming preached, "Boost the soil and the environment around the vines, and everything will be fine." I decided to remove all the diseased vines and replant with new ones that were grafted onto phylloxera-resistant rootstocks. It sounded like an easy solution: Get rid of the diseased vines and the problem will go away. My logic, and that of those I adopted it from, was that if I took away all infested vines and planted a new vineyard I would be better off because the longer I waited the longer I would be without a productive farm. In hindsight I wonder why I gave in to this illogical reasoning when my vines were still producing some crop; I was in fact still making money off my fruit.

* * *

I'll never forget the day the vines were ripped out—the chainsaws, the crews marching through my vineyard lopping off the tops of my grapevines and haphazardly tossing them into large piles. The last three years of compassion and love I had poured into them were gone in an instant, and so was the joy and energy they had given. The smell was sickening, the visuals horrifying, and even though it seemed so wrong, I didn't know what else to do. I had convinced myself that the answer to the problem was to replant with new, resistant young vines, like replacing a lost dog with a new puppy. Rachel, Grace, Dude, and Joy surrounded me and held tight to me as the vines were taken away. All of us had a sinking feeling as we watched the destruction unfold before us on an otherwise gorgeous September afternoon.

We parked ourselves on the soil of the vineyard as dusk approached and talked about how fine life would be when my 5,300 new Merlot grapevines arrived the next day. After researching the three or so different Merlot clone types available to me, categorized by their different wine qualities and points of origin, I chose a clone 3. This clone came from Inglenook Winery (and before that probably France), and had been renamed by University of California at Davis after being tested and shown to be disease-free. I believed that its richness of character embodied my beliefs for a successful wine. The Merlot vines were to be grafted (grapevines consist of two parts: the stock or roots, and the scion or fruit variety of the vine) onto a rootstock called 110R, which is resistant to phylloxera, hearty to drought conditions, and loves to grow on hillsides—per-

BUYING GRAPEVINES

Nurseries off different options

GREENVINES

They are grafted in the winter around February and are delivered as early as May. Planting should be done after the threat of frost is over.

ONE YEAR BIG POT BENCH GRAFTS

Optimal planting after threat of frost in the early spring or up to fall for a better chance of good growth for the next year.

fect characteristics for my area. Nevermind the diseased stumps that stood every six feet in rows eight feet apart. The fresh vines were to be planted in between the stumps of the old vines, which would be removed later, using the same row configuration. The newfangled would soon mask the ugliness and disturbing look of the old. The kids drank sparkling grape juice and Rachel and I drank a Rafanelli Cabernet Sauvignon that I had carefully saved from a winery tour I'd taken in my enology class the previous fall. Rafanelli is a small winery where the fruit is hand picked and, of the 9,000-or-so cases produced each year, nearly sixty percent of the bottles are sold out the door to visiting wine drinkers and those "in the know."

The wine was lively and reminded me of how inspiring the tour had been as we climbed around the hillside in Dry Creek Valley and watched as the owner David Rafanelli and his crew painstakingly planted vines on a steep cliff that overlooked the valley. Most growers would have felt threatened by planting grapes on land like that, but not them. Even though they knew it to be challenging, they also realized that the fruit would be one-of-a-kind. The Rafanelli wine was my encouragement that day with its fruity hint of success and flavorful struggle. I wasn't facing any of their challenges—erosion issues, trellis adaptability, and harvest difficulties. I laid back and allowed myself to enjoy the lovely September day; it was a good time for us to plant the one-year-old big pot bench graft vines I'd ordered, and I comforted myself with the thought that I would have none of their land problems later on. The Rafanelli Cabernet was exactly what I needed to christen the future planting of my vines. In retrospect, that kind of success in farming doesn't come without hard work and many mistakes.

They say you learn from your mistakes, and for me this was certainly true. *How could the vines I'd planted to replace the phylloxera-ridden vines be unhealthy and sickly?* I asked myself. This couldn't be happening. But I was a newcomer, I realized, who had to learn everything I knew from a set of rules that had been assembled, usually randomly, from nothing more than my own anguish and an instinctual need to succeed. Other farmers, whom I envied, had the doctrines of their parents and their grandparents. They had generations of expertise and logs of past years. They had the wisdom to know that farming is a passion that starts deep within your soul and permeates every orifice of your spirit, a way of life that can't be feigned or simulated, something that develops through time and is a result of nothing more than hardship and generations of sweat. I

FARMING STYLES

My Old Style of Farming for Fall

Strip-spraying chemicals below the grapevines, then disking the weeds in the middle of vine rows.

My New Style of Farming for Fall

Since I couldn't start raising cows for the purpose of fertilization, nor could I have horses to cultivate manure, I began using another organic approach one where I would need to bring in organics and cultivate them on my own.

"Organic," in a farming context, means using the byproducts from plants and animals as a means to provide necessary nutrients for the growth and continued support of living plants. The nutrients released from the organic matter are decomposed by microorganisms within the soil and then become available for the living plant—my grapevines.

Compost

Whether purchased or homemade, compost is filled with

only knew that I was afraid of failing, and that I was desperate to clear away the phylloxera problem.

Because of my perceived failure, and because I was desperate for answers and couldn't control the unwanted chaos of my farming mis-

animal and plant byproducts and provides nutrients and microorganisms for cover crops and soil.

Cover Crops

Cover cropping (planting only in between the grapevines—not underneath them) improves soil structure and water penetration, adds organic matter, and adds microorganisms: bacteria, fungi, earthworms, arthropods.

There are many different types of cover crops that can be planted, and there are no set rules on exactly what to plant. The important thing to remember is that legumes will produce nitrogen (needed for growth of the vine) and grasses will hinder the growth of other unwanted plants, help with erosion, tie up nitrogen, and make the area pretty. If vines are overly vigorous and fruit crop is poor, then the cover crop needs to be adjusted. The grower needs to watch the vines and make adjustments according to how the vines are responding. Each year the formula may change.

takes, I started searching for answers to my farming problems. I dug into the recesses of my memory, like a gardener shoveling away debris, and I accessed memories I wasn't sure I wanted to remember. The truth was hidden in the recessed archives of my brain, and my creative thoughts on farming came to me as I followed a string of memories into the realm of the forgotten doctrines of my past. I was ten years old, my long braids carefully tied with pink ribbons, sitting on a bench at lunchtime eating my sandwich. My mother's constant quest for health food set me apart from my peers. While everyone enjoyed their Wonder Bread sandwiches, I was stuck with sprouted, nutty, grainy tasteless sandwiches that no one envied. Euell Gibbons was her idol—famous for his Post Grape Nut cereal commercials that my brother, sister, and I constantly ridiculed. We teased her endlessly, mimicking Euell and his earthy, back-to-nature slogans.

As an older, wiser daughter, I realize she was ahead of the trend and had our health as her primary interest. When she was fixating on Gibbons's teachings and taking cooking classes in Berkeley with renowned and innovative chefs like Alice Waters and Joyce Goldstein, I was getting my first lesson on wholesome eating and the benefits of using organic, natural products. "If you don't eat healthy foods, then your body won't be healthy," she said. "You are what you eat."

Why had I forgotten all this? Why did I think that if I fed my grapevines unhealthy foods my vines would be healthy? Although I'd known about the differences between things like composting, synthetically fertilizing, and doing nothing to the soil, I hadn't realized the dramatic impact those differences could really have on my vineyard.

I also thought about and started focusing on how the seasons and their cycles might affect this process. How do untouched forests and virgin mountain regions function without the involvement of man? The four seasons and their cycles provide the forests with all they need to maintain the complex balance of nature and promote

76

HOW TO COMPOST AND COVER CROP SEVEN ACRES

Compost: Applied October–November, 3 tons/acre
Cover Crop: Applied in Fall When Expecting Rainfall

LEGUMES (ADD NITROGEN)

- Crimson clover: 10 pounds per acre (brings nitrogen)

- Bell bean: 50 pounds per acre (aerates soil, brings beneficial insects)

- Magnus pea: 40 pounds per acre (encourages biomass)

GRASSES (REDUCE EROSION, TIES UP NITROGEN)

- Oats: 50 pounds per acre

- Mustard: 10 pounds per acre

Compost: Applied October–November

- mix in approximately 30–50% volume of the area being planted

  or

- put 1–2 pounds compost in each hole before planting new vines

  or

- dig in 1–2 inches of compost a couple of feet around the vine, and mix it 2–3 inches down each year after vines are planted

---

▷

Cover Crop: Applied in Fall
When Expecting Rainfall

- dig up the area to be planted, add some water, turn soil twice over a 2-week period, and seed (using a combination of legumes and grasses)

   or

- ask you local seed dealer for a good combination

   or

- allow your weeds to grow and then manage the natural vegetation by mowing and digging under in the early

---

the growth of our unchanged forests; shouldn't this be the same for any farming we do?

The seasons work their magic. In the fall, after the grapevines' leaves drop to the ground, they decompose. The decomposition process is aided by the bacteria and worms on the ground, and by certain elements within the structure of the leaves. The grapevine bulks up with these decomposed nutrients and begins turning its energy inward, getting ready to shut down for the winter. While the vine is dormant and resting, the soil remains alive with microorganisms that continue working to break down available nutrients that the vine will use once spring arrives. In late winter, weeds and wildflowers begin a self-reseeding process, as they germinate and regenerate from seeds dropped to the ground after the previous growing season. Spring arrives and the grapevine begins a period of breathtaking growth, aided by the available nutrients stored in the winter soil. The energy of the vine is directed outward, as the fruit begins maturation. The wildflowers and weeds begin dying off, dropping their leaves and flowers onto the ground, decomposing and generating more nutrients for the vine's fruit development. The summer sun ripens the fruit, the fruit falls, and the yearly cycle begins again.

I was beginning to understand that if I disrupted this process—using chemicals and synthetic fertilizers—the cycle would be interrupted, the harmony disbanded, and the clarity transformed into an imperfect image that bewilders the observer (in plain terms: dead soil and unhealthy plants). I had been a sufferer of this very thing, a victim of my own ignorance, and an observer who overlooked the need for all the parts to function together as one whole. I had made the devastating mistake of ripping out vines and replanting with new ones only to find that my problem was not about the vines themselves; it was about what I was feeding them and the unhappy soil they were growing in.

I didn't invent these simple farming concepts. I had forgotten many important, relevant parts of my past, things I most needed to fall back on. Past generations of wise farmers (and my mother), and great philosophers like Aristotle, who said, "Nature does nothing uselessly," were my motivation for changing my practices that fifth fall of farming. Twenty years ago, while I was studying rhetoric at the University of California at Berkeley, I was inundated with these ideas. But I had forgotten about those college farming papers I wrote. I had forgotten about my mother's infamous treks to find organic food products—even when they weren't findable—and her basic philosophy about eating wild edibles and her indelible desire to feed us foods that would make us healthy. It turned out that fall was the season that guided me toward the decision to trade in the old-fashioned for a new mode of farming—one that was practical, conscientious, and visionary. It was time for me to start over and begin anew with a fresh perspective. My new goal was to learn how to farm successfully by maintaining the health and balance of the environment around me, using little or nothing more than the power of the season, meanwhile promoting the health of the soil and the ecosystem.

To this day my mother still thinks about going on her wild edible escapades. This past Thanksgiving she pulled out a recipe that called for "one Norwegian spruce branch."

"Did you get it, Mom?" I asked. I knew she hadn't gone to Norway but I wondered if she had ordered a cutting over the phone, or perhaps the Internet, and had it delivered to her doorstep. I was disappointed to hear that she had omitted the branch entirely. "Couldn't you have used a local pine tree branch instead?" I joked, laughing to myself about good 'ole Euell.

But I'm not laughing now, because I learned that sometimes things make sense long after the fact. She had the answer to the problem long before anyone else.

Winter

Wine is the most civilized thing in the world.
—*Ernest Hemingway*

WINTER IN PARIS

2011

I am in the Louvre. But I am not here to view artwork; I am here to pour wine. The twenty of us stand erect in a line, perfectly coiffed in matching black suits, each carrying a tray holding twenty sparkling glasses filled halfway with white wine. The velvet curtain we stand behind is quickly pulled open, and the first in line marches through the entrance as Monsieur Ramage paces up and down the line, reminding us to smile and stand up straight. This is the beginning of our day, and although it's exciting at first, the routine gets old quickly, especially because this is the second day of two fifteen-hour shifts.

It's wine o'clock. This becomes a standard joke after the first day of Le Grand Tasting. I have just returned to Paris after having spent three days in New York for Thanksgiving with my family. I slept the entire eight-hour plane ride, totally exhausted from the quick jaunt to the States. Paris was a dismal gray when I land at Orly Airport. Training for Le Grand Tasting began in September, when we learned that we would be serving some of the most renowned French wines to journalists and wine aficionados from around the world for the two-day December event at Le Louvre, an event that began in 2006 to showcase premier wines of France.

Initially, it sounded like it was going to be easy, but as December 2 approached, the tension among the students rose. We spent weeks of class time learning how to properly open wine and carry a tray full of twenty glasses without making a sound. An obstacle course was set up for this training, with chairs randomly placed to obstruct our pathway to our make-believe judges. The top contenders were the students who could weave through the course and climb over the chairs without spilling a drop of wine or clanging their glasses on the tray. The training was meant to build our self-confidence, but instead it created more anxiety.

We have memorized the correct serving temperatures for each variety of wine and the rules of carafing and decanting, and we've gone over and over the perfect demeanor for a server, which we must display on these two precious fifteen-hour days at the Carousel du Louvre. Some 120 producers of the finest French wines have come together—Chateau Lafite, Chateau Margaux, and Krug Champagne, to name a few—all here to impress hundreds of tasters and journalists from the international world of wine.

Not only were we required to learn about decanting and the proper serving temperatures for different wines, but we also had to learn to decipher the conundrum of whether to carafe or not to carafe. And why must we be so bloody obsessed with the protocol of carafing, decanting, and correct serving temperatures? At first these rules seemed silly, considering we had to memorize all the Grand

Crus of Burgundy as well as the Premier Crus for each AOC in Burgundy and Bordeaux. We also had to learn Bordeaux's different and complicated wine-ranking system, and then we had to learn about the other regions of France and the other wine-producing countries of the world. But during Le Grand Tasting, I reacquaint myself with the reasons for tradition and protocol when it comes to temperature and carafing and decanting wines: It all stems around the pleasure gained from a particular vintage of wine when it is properly served.

It is an honor to present wine at Le Grand Tasting, and yet I hoped that I would not be one of the chosen students to chill and serve. I hoped to only assist. But my plans were thwarted when Monsieur Ramage assigned me Chateau Doisy-Daene, Clos Floridene, presented by its proprietor Denis Dubourdieu. So today I am in charge of four expensive vintages: Graves Clos Floridene, rouge 2005; Graves Clos Floridene, blanc 2009; Graves Clos Floridene, blanc 2001; and Graves Chateau Doisy-Daene, blanc 1945. I must now decide proper temperatures and whether to carafe, decant, or do nothing, and I must present these wines to the hundreds of critics that are in attendance at Le Louvre.

Everything must be carefully calculated using traditional French rules about wine temperature, which include an intricate three-hour pre-chilling process. My scheduled serving time is 6:00 PM on December 3, so I will begin the process at 3:00 PM. But when I arrive, I learn that the tasting is running late, so I must now take this into account in preparing my perfect wine temperatures. As I begin my work, I realize the infrared thermometer has disappeared again, and I run through the large kitchen and cooling lockers searching for the sophisticated temperature gauge.

Why is it so important to serve wine at the right temperature?

Again, it has to do with aromas. Different aromas are brought out at different temperatures for different wines. If a wine is too cold or too warm, it can lose certain aromas and flavors that are specific to the character of that particular wine. One July, for example, I foolishly served my 2007 award-winning Midnight Moulton Cabernet after the bottle had been rolling around in the hot trunk of my car for three days. The tannins, brought forth from the heat, overpowered the notable qualities of the fruit, and my crowd of interested wine fans quickly dispersed.

When certain wines, especially red wines, are served too warm, the taste of alcohol can be overpowering, and the dominant flavor can be an acetic burn. If red wine is over-chilled, it can taste astringent, or sharp and tart, from the tannins becoming overemphasized. It all boils down to finding a mid-range temperature that achieves the perfect balance of fruit, alcohol, and tannin and doesn't stifle the structure of the wine.

But there is no time to waste and no mid-range temperature allowed for the serving of my wines today at Le Louvre. Preparation begins when I open all thirty-two bottles and begin loading large plastic bins with buckets of ice, water, wet towels, and, of course, the eight bottles of each of the four vintages of wine. The more ice and less water I have in the bins, the faster I can drop the temperatures. If I need to slow the temperature from dropping too rapidly, I can add more water to the ice.

I pull out my list from my apron pocket and search for the notes I have taken on the proper temperatures for each of my wines. This is only the beginning, as the key is in checking and rechecking all thirty-two bottles every three minutes or so on a rotating basis (for nearly two hours) to make sure that the temperatures are a couple of degrees colder than my optimum serving temperature. We do this so that once they are poured into the glasses and marched to the judges, their temperature will be perfect. The problem is in knowing the exact moment to launch the pouring because there are constantly delays and changes in schedule throughout the event.

The 1945 vintage becomes a nightmare when the cork breaks and I can't get it out. My classmates circle me and beg to open the next bottle. When I acquiesce, one classmate not only breaks the cork, but also pushes it into the bottle. I take back control, realizing that I must be responsible whether or not I fail.

The temperatures at which I must serve my wines are as follows: Graves Clos Floridene, rouge 2005, 18° C or 64.4° F; Graves Clos Floridene, blanc 2009, 9° C or 48.2° F; Graves Clos Floridene, blanc 2001, 9° C or 48.2° F, and Graves Chateau Doisy-Daene, blanc 1945, 11° C or 51.8° F.

In addition to chilling the wine to the correct temperature, I must also decide whether to decant, carafe, or neither. Decanting is a traditional and integral part of old-style wine service. A decanter is normally a beautiful glass piece that is wide at the bottom and narrow through the neck, and which sometimes has a stopper. It is used to clarify and remove the sediment that can accumulate in an older bottle of wine. Sediment needs to be removed because it can produce bitter and unpleasant flavors. However, older and more fragile wines need to be handled gently, and pouring them into a decanter can cause them to be over-aerated, which can result in

TEMPERATURES

Bordeaux: 65° F, 18° C	**Red Burgundy:** 63° F, 17° C
Chablis: 48°–53° F, 9°–12° C	**Riesling:** 47° F, 8° C
Champagne: 38°–45° F,	**Rioja:** 61° F, 16° C
3°–7° C	**Rose:** 45°–50° F, 7°–10° C
Chardonnay: 48°–52° F,	**Sauternes:** 52° F, 11° C
9°–11° C	**Sauvignon Blanc:** 48°–53° F,
Chianti: 59° F, 15° C	9°–12° C
Ice Wines: 43° F, 6° C	**Shiraz:** 65° F, 18° C
Pinot Noir: 61° F, 16° C	**Viognier:** 52° F, 11° C
Port: 65°–70° F, 18°–21° C	**Zinfandel:** 59° F, 15° C

oxidation and thereby produce a wine that is tannic, fruitless, and has an overabundance of oak.

Carafing is usually used to aerate wines. Normally a carafe is more open at the neck, allowing the wine consumer to see the wine, and it is a great way to open up the flavors of a young wine. It can also be a great tool to help judge whether an old wine needs to be decanted or not.

Here's the big secret when it comes to deciding whether or not to use a carafe: smell, smell, smell. Pour a small amount of wine into your glass. If the first smell (before you swirl the wine) and the second smell (after you swirl the wine) produce the same aromas, then the wine is structurally balanced and ready to drink without carafing. If the first smell has few aromas but the second smell, after swirling, opens the aromas up, then the wine is young and needs to be carafed and aerated in order to bring out flavors and control harsh tannins and tightness. Finally, if there are many aromas on the first whiff but none after swirling the glass, then the wine is old and may not need carafing, though it will probably need careful decanting to remove sediment.

At the Louvre on the day of my presentation, I carefully decant my 1945 vintage to remove the particles of cork and bits of old-age sediment without disturbing the fragility of the wine. After tasting my other wines, I decide that the whites do not need to be carafed because they are structurally balanced, meaning the first smell is consistent with the second smell after aeration. My 2005 red varietal, still quite young for a French red wine, needs some opening and release of its flavor and complexity, so I decide to carafe it for about thirty minutes.

Ultimately, it's all about finding the sweet spot, or the perfect time and temperature at which to drink a particular wine wine; however, by sticking to temperatures best suited to a variety, and considering whether a wine needs aeration in carafing or decanting for sediment removal, a wine connoisseur can be ahead of the game. The goal is to serve a wine with perfect structure—a balance of fruit, tannins, and alcohols. Understanding that wine changes because of age, serving conditions, and variety is the key to making this happen. These are the mysteries that contribute to the beauty of wine, which endlessly intrigues the passions and palates of wine aficionados worldwide.

Six o'clock arrives at the Louvre, and my wines are poured and served. Monsieur Ramage has randomly checked the trays for precision and correct temperature and has given me a thumbs-up and a giant smile. The curtain opens for the last delivery of wine, and I take a deep breath as I smile to myself and march before the judges for a final round of applause.

FIVE

LIFE IS LIKE A BOTTLE OF WINE, YOU NEVER KNOW WHAT VINTAGE YOU'RE GONNA GET

2003

I love the sparkle of winter: the sounds that rise during a flashy storm, the Herculean explosions that roll through the valley, and the calm that arrives once the upheaval is over. Sometimes, if we're lucky, we see the translucent flicker of snow. I treasure this wintertime solstice picture show when the vine shuts down for the winter, the wild animals prepare for hibernation, the grasses die off, and the trees become barren, simply because the countryside takes on a minimalist appearance.

When Rachel first arrived she was perplexed by my lack of early winter preparation. "Shouldn't you be unpacking your sweaters from the attic and dismantling your cartons of gloves, hats, and boots?" she casually inquired in her authoritative British accent.

"Nope," I said, "I keep my sweaters on hooks placed around the house and my boots tucked conspicuously in a corner of the kitchen." She had already noticed this when she'd arrived, and it had bothered her.

"It's untraditional and slovenly," she had told me late one night after a few glasses of wine. But I soon impressed upon her that there are times—even during the heat of the summer—when taking care of the land requires use of these winterlike articles.

"I've needed my winter gear, and not had to look for it, and besides, life is like a box of chocolates, you never know what you're gonna get!" I told her. This truism is especially relevant when you squish through muddy pools of water in the summer after discovering a leak in your well, septic, or irrigation lines, or when you take a brisk late evening walk in the vineyard in search of wild animals munching on the leaves or fruit of your grapevines.

And although it's true that winter brings mental relief from being a slave to many sleepless nights where I wake up wondering if my precious fruit is getting what it needs, and praying that rain won't come too early and shatter my bloom or rot my crop, and that disease and vermin won't destroy my prolific harvest, I've taken it upon myself to make winter a time of arduous physical work. Rather than soak up the last flicker of dropping grape leaves as they carry away the past year's happiness and grief and take heed from nature to rest and forget about yesteryear, I dance my way through the season inventing wayward procedures for managing the land on my farm.

In the beginning, I promised myself that I would never poison, maim, emotionally abuse, or kill any animal; unfortunately, I have committed all of these immoral acts. I rationalize my behavior by telling you I had it all backwards, and that at the time I felt forced to—that is, there was no future for me in farming if I didn't "buck up" by removing all unwanted vermin and focusing only on the subject at hand—my grape crop.

I remember a viticulture class one winter when I had flinched as a ground squirrel darted by my booted foot, almost tripping me as I climbed on the tractor. One of the more macho students called out, "What are you afraid of, Moulton? Those creatures have a right to live here. They provide the diversity needed to maintain a healthy farm." *Oh, brother,* I thought to myself, *now we have an intellectual speech from the macho farmer.* Though I knew he was kidding, I wondered how a ground squirrel or a snake or a bird could help keep a farm healthy? From my city point of view, a city bird was useful only when posing for a picture with Golden Gate Park in the background.

He continued, pointing out that if I eliminated all my gophers, the barn owls would go elsewhere for food; if I obliterated all my ground squirrels, the eagles, coyotes, gopher snakes, and rattlesnakes would disappear in search of food. Animals were needed for a healthy ecosystem on my farm because their excrement provided my soil with bacteria and microorganisms necessary for decomposing nutrients. I needed at least some of these animals to encourage a healthy food chain on my property in order to procure these benefits.

Logically, I could understand this concept. I had already learned the hard way about the importance of keeping my soil alive. Even so, from the moment we stepped onto our country property, I still believed that the way to survive in an existence overwrought with the excessive freedoms of nature was to control and manage that environment. This approach had followed me from the manicured, suburban lifestyle of my childhood where it was easy to remove gophers and weed a ten-foot-square piece of land. But living in the country was different; it wasn't so easy to weed twenty-four acres of rolling hills and remove acres of wild animals, many of whom were chomping away at my grapevines.

Because I was so busy trying to adjust to all the fresh, unforeseen situations, I lost my vision and original theories about maintaining the health of my ecosystem by using natural methods and not tempering with the land. And it took many moons of howling coyotes and wild turkeys parading through my home before I was able to forget about my own selfish needs and focus once again on my original goals. It was like not being able to see the forest through the trees; the daily toil blinded me.

* * *

One of the worst crimes I committed was the beheading of a beautiful snake. The snake was bothering my land, I thought. Actually, I didn't personally do the job; I issued the orders to have the job done by my vineyard helpers. This atrocious beheading proved not only terminal for the snake, but debilitating to the health of my farm. While the assailant prepared for the event, his assistant sat ten feet away taking a comfortable break away from the action. I came to my bedroom window to see if they had finished when I saw the man who had been sitting up on his feet with a startled look on his face. His friend was pointing and laughing hysterically.

I watched as the man who had carried out the act ran toward the house, shovel in hand; seconds later the doorbell rang. I answered it, wondering if his friend had been startled from witnessing the event. He stood at the doorstep and in his broken English explained to me that his friend needed a break. Interspersed with a grin and small giggles he said he wasn't feeling well. I learned that the force of the shovel and the size of the body sent the snake's head flying many feet into the air, landing it precisely on the bystander's lap—the tongue still flapping and eyes twitching. "Sure," I grimaced at him. "No problem, tell him to take all the time he needs." I glimpsed through the window on my way back through the house and saw the man lying flat on his back with his eyes shut and a tortured expression on his face.

Many days later, I was sitting in the hairdresser's listening to my hair stylist talk about a rattler his son had found at their house—just that morning. I thought nothing of it until the forest ranger showed up at the beauty parlor with the snake safely placed in a glass jar. "It's like door-to-door delivery service," the ranger said. "I thought you might like to see that baby rattler you called about, and decided to swing on by and show it to you," motioning in the direction of my hair stylist.

"Gee, thanks," we all said. "What a nice surprise." The lady sitting in the chair beside me quipped, "We can have our hair done and feel like we're in the reptile hall at the zoo." We all laughed.

I chimed in with a description of the snake that had recently been mutilated on my property. I detailed its physical traits, thinking how great it was to have a captive forest ranger at a place where one would least expect it. Regrettably, he did not say what I thought he would say, "If you see it again, you better leave it alone." He explained that the kind of snake I had described, a king snake, should never be killed since it hunts rodents and other poisonous snakes.

"Maybe, I mean, I saw a snake that looks vaguely like that ... err, a while ago," I lied, swallowing my words and muttering under my breath

A slap in the face would have hurt less.

That lesson on killing the snake stuck with me until I had more frustrating events with animals. Learning something once just wasn't quite enough to make an impression on me. I had to learn it again, and again, and again.

✳ ✳ ✳

The learning started anew when deer decided to feast on my ripe grapes. I had carefully saved a couple of rows of crop in order to make my own wine, leaving the rest for the contracted winery. There were to be fifty people arriving on a Saturday afternoon to pick, stomp, and party in celebration of the fruit. The festivities had been finalized and there was one day left before commencement. Up to that point I had kept a close watch on the vines making sure that no birds, animals, or humans destroyed this intended tribute to Mother Nature. But from one evening to the next morning the deer had completely eaten four long rows of grapes.

I nearly choked when I saw the destruction they wreaked in a single night of gorging on fruit. In my ignorance I had missed certain indications that deer had already sized up my grapes and were merely waiting for the perfect time to dine on the ripe fruit. They began their process slowly and methodically by sampling certain areas of grapes each night. In the busy preparation of the party, I hadn't seen their tracks and I hadn't seen their scat. Deer seem to know exactly when the sugars are perfect and, come to think of it, they may be a better indicator of when to harvest than any gadget used to test sugars. According to them, we had hit the perfect time to harvest. And contrary to belief, deer around here are not shy; instead, they are brazen, sneaky, and very rambunctious. They put the lithe bobcats and spry mountain lions to shame with their tenacious virtues and talented perceptions of where to find the best food.

Because of their less-than-desirable personality traits, and because I was tired of my revenue being digested in the gut of an animal, I decided to make it my goal to remove deer from the vineyard, especially during the winter, long before they became a threat to the springtime leaves. Since there are large numbers of deer to evacuate, winter suddenly becomes very busy around my home. I spend a good portion of my time inventing different maneuvers in order to remove them, including stalking, beebee gun in hand, at different times of the night hoping to catch them unawares. Like an angry trapper pursuing an aggressive bear caught ravaging through his stored food, I furiously pursue those deer.

Outmaneuvering them involves quite a lot of creativity on my part, since I can't bring myself to permanently rid myself of them, ever since the snake incident. I just have to do it in a manner that soothes my psyche and allows me to later harvest a substantial crop. My tactics *don't* frighten the deer away. I learned that because they always seemed to come back. I think they got used to my presence; they expected my visits. One evening in particular, I actually thought I'd won the battle. As I approached a group of deer, they all scattered and ran in different directions. *Voila*, I thought, *they finally know who's boss around here.* When I turned to head back home, I saw what I thought looked like a coyote standing behind a tree, his coat freely blowing in the wind. I didn't know whether to shoot, run, or climb an oak tree. I knew I didn't want to mess with that creature, ever—with or without a beebee gun. I abandoned my late evening exercise altogether, and though it's made my nights much more pleasant, I also had to give into the fact that the coyote, or whatever it was, deserved credit for scattering the deer that night.

I now ward off deer by another means that I call the Scarecrow Method. You probably think I'm referring to a stuffed figure wearing bright color clothing and a silly hat attached to a post placed somewhere in the vicinity of the grapevines. But I'm a hands-on kind of gal, so my method entails my car and a frightening and haggard image driving my car—namely me. I casually drive to the entrance of the vineyard and quietly wait, with the lights and engine of my car turned off. At the first spotting of deer, I quickly flash my high beams, hit the gas, lay my hand on the horn, and chase them through the vineyard serenading profanities. This technique sends the deer running in all directions and they usually hop over the fence and bounce away. I haven't injured them; merely relocated them to a place more conducive to their lifestyle. I use this approach many nights a week, unless my children, who are intolerant of this stalking routine, happen to be with me. "Not tonight, Mom, please!" they cry impatiently. They do not share my same concerns about protecting the grapes.

I also discovered, by accident during the course of all my creative attempts to get rid of the deer, that another successful way to deter them is to plant roses—many roses—near the grapevines. Deer love roses. Instead of attacking the fruit they prefer to munch on sweet, fresh roses. But this solution will only work during rose-blooming season and once the roses are gone the deer will move on to munching foliage and fruit from the vines.

Deer are one of the biggest and most feared animal culprit in number and size and cause the greatest amount of damage to grapevines. Grapevines provide nourishment for deer in all grape-growing regions. Deer munching away on foliage causes severe weakening of new vines and prevents fruiting on older vines (it takes sixteen to twenty leaves per shoot to ripen two clusters of grapes). And once the crop is actually ripe they can consume copious amounts of grapes in a very short period of time. They are very sneaky in that they come out at night to feed and hide in the bushes during the day. The red flag you want to watch out for is vines that are stripped of their foliage, and empty stems left on the vine just before harvest.

There are an inexhaustible amount of books and pamphlets written on the problem of removing deer and unwieldy animals from your home, your garden, or your farm. I've studied many of them, and most of them paint a pleasant picture of the virtues of poisons, not mentioning anything about natural remedies such as my Scarecrow Method, planting roses, blasting music, or spraying the repellent panther pee. They don't tell you the ramifications of using poisonous products nor the complicated aftereffects associated with their use.

✳ ✳ ✳

I tried the poison approach once. I felt, at the time, that it was the best option for me because my farmland had left me searching for quick solutions, and there was extreme urgency in my need. While most plants, animals, and even humans are preparing for their winter dormancy or rest period, the animals around here grow energetic and exuberant. Instead of winding down for the winter, I found myself chasing what turned out to be an opossum from under my kitchen floor. The scratching noise started around dusk and continued until dawn. After successfully denying the sound for three days, I could no longer ignore it when a hole the size of a nickel appeared in my kitchen floor. I decided to find a pointy stick, shove it through the hole, and hopefully scare away the creature making all the racket. The stick not only didn't alarm the animal, it in fact seemed to motivate him. His clawed foot shot through the hole and moved around in a strange gesture that I didn't take to be a warm greeting.

My husband's solution to the situation was to poison the animal. We argued about this approach, but in the end I lost. I watched him pour warfarin, an anticoagulant used to kill rodents, through the nickel-size hole. I knew the outcome would be bad.

A week later a seeping combination of rotten eggs, mold, and bad fish penetrated our kitchen. The animal had died, either from the puncture wounds I bestowed on him or from the poison Chuck had poured down the hole. The dead animal's stench was more than we could bear, and no one wanted to volunteer to stick a hand down there to remove it. Ultimately, I turned to bribing my only son. Dude, hero that he is, cheerfully took the job when promised enough candy to last him an entire year. At the ripe age of seven he seemed just perfect for the job. Fully clad in a jumpsuit and mask, with flashlight in hand (looking much the same as he might if he were going to the moon), he stepped into the crawlspace under our refrigerator. We all stood around in anticipation, begging him to rid us of the awful odor, using our most persuasive words to coax him and make him feel good about the task we had so unkindly asked him to do.

Grace cheered him on, telling him he could sit in the front seat of the car for the next month. Joy giggled and stuttered, telling him he could have her favorite stuffed animal and he wouldn't have to read her a bedtime story ever again. We were desperate, believe me, each of us trying to woo him in our own special way. But to no avail. Whether it was the darkness, or the dust clouding his vision, or the wind whistling through the crawlspace, our attempts were thwarted and my son emerged from the hole without having sighted the animal. He murmured something about dark shadows and bones. It was a brave attempt.

I suddenly had an awakening about numerous unpleasant odors we had tried to outrun in the past. I thought about why we had spent so much of our time wallowing about the house in search of a fresh-smelling place to eat our meals and rest ourselves. We had used poisons before. It was evidenced by the hundreds of bone remnants Dude found under the floorboards.

The awful smell in our country kitchen did finally dissipate, and we could once again enjoy an evening without the promiscuous stench of death. But as the stink was disappearing, the birds were appearing. Between the nervy deer, the howling coyotes, and the vile opossums, there was no place for us to go to get away from the animal life. It seemed that our space was their space. On another particular evening, another unrestful twilight, a very large wild turkey wandered through the front door while I was unloading the groceries. Not to be confused with a buzzard or vulture, this turkey was the kind of bird one might see as the centerpiece of an American Thanksgiving celebration. Wild turkeys are large and peacock-like, especially when they open their brightly colored plumage. They also inhabit our property and aren't at all fussed about sharing the front yard, the backyard, the vineyard, and, that evening, the house.

I couldn't use my gun. I'd already decided killing animals didn't suit my motives for coexisting peacefully with the wildlife on our property, and I couldn't use poisons. I wasn't willing to deal with any incriminating family finger-pointing once the odor from the dead animal arrived. This didn't leave me with much to select from, and maybe I just should have given up at this point and opened a zoo for exotic animals. But giving up was not within my realm of possibilities. I have too much pride to let my children see me quit or falter in any way. I was the teacher with my children in tow, and if I made the wrong choices that would certainly be what they always remembered. I didn't want that.

As the wild turkey wandered through our home, Bubba, our wonderful twenty-five pound canine beast, who we had acquired to replace Sha-na-na and who was compact and docile (and hated the outdoors so much that Chuck never worried again about me breaking my ankle in search of him in the blackness of night), was petrified and not willing to remove himself from his hiding place under the kitchen table. Grace and Joy screamed hysterically as Dude presented me with his frog net. I grabbed the net, purchased from the local toy store for butterfly catching, and headed for the bird that was running down hallways, having a grand time exploring its new territory.

There was no way I could catch that large a bird in so little a net, and even if I did the bird would break through the fine netting in a matter of seconds. Turkeys actually fly, and this one had mastered the technique of running and flying at the same time. I contemplated grabbing its claws when it took off in flight, but decided against this when I realized how sharp they were. The disturbed bird just stared at us with a blank, wild-eyed gaze as we dashed about trying to persuade him back to the forest. Like sheep-herding dogs moving a group of cattle, Dude and I finally drove the bird toward an open doorway. In a matter of minutes we had the turkey moved to a place where it could run to the outside and catch up with its flock.

But the fact that it had left our home and was headed for the vineyard would present a big problem later. Wild turkeys and many other birds like to feed on grapes; in fact, most birds love grapes, especially sweet, ripe grapes that are ready to be picked and turned into wine. They don't eat the entire grape berry; they merely deflate it, leaving portions of the cluster intact. Although the destruction that birds cause may seem slight, it can result in secondary problems that compound the damage. As the birds peck away on the grape and the berry begins to ooze, fungus enters through the tear and you end up with a grape cluster that is smelly, rotten, and completely worthless. And it doesn't only destroy that cluster; if it gets near any other clusters the fungus can travel and damage even more fruit.

❊   ❊   ❊

Since I thought that protecting my fruit crop was my biggest goal, all of my ludicrous attempts to control the animals on my property didn't seem wrong to me. They just seemed like the way to survive life on a farm. And although I'd nearly killed animals, used scare tactics, and inflicted emotional abuse, I still hadn't learned what I needed to know in order to live successfully in the country. What more was left?

The final reckoning came when it was too cold to go outside and the animals living around or in my house were driving me crazy. In an effort to attempt one last time to rid my home of animal scratching, arguing, and mischief, I called a "consultant" to help me determine if there might be a way to outsmart and remove the animals living in and around my home and vineyard. As we tromped through the muddy areas around the exterior of our house searching for any signs of the animals, we happened upon an odd thing—a crawl space access area had been kicked in, the screen removed, and the door left ajar.

We peered into the dark hole leading under the house, and for a split second everything was calm. A large animal, squealing and angry, came flying out with the speed of a tomahawk. We both flew back with such great force that we ended up on top of one another. Once we'd regained our composure, he gently informed me that I should contact the police and have them make a report before any trapping could be done. "The smashed in door could have been from one of your kids," he said, "but surely you would have known if one of them had been injured." There was a chewed up hat and a bloody sock that looked like it had been used as a tourniquet laying on the ground. The articles looked like they'd been left by someone who was in a grand hurry. That was the last time I ever saw the trapper.

Since my last encounter with the police had been anything but pleasurable, I hated to call them for any type of service, whether it be fear of darkness and isolation or this more serious crime, breaking and entering. But I swallowed my pride for the sake of my children and telephoned the police asking to speak with any officer except the one who had already counseled me on the "safeness" of my home.

The officer was quite pleased with his assessment of the situation. "I know you don't want to hear this, Missy (there was that name again), but it looks pretty clear to me."

"It does?" I responded, in a disbelieving voice.

"Yes," he said. "There are footprints and signs of a struggle, not with a human, but with an animal."

"Really?" I puzzled, disbelieving that the animal who had just charged our faces was the real culprit. "Hmm," I let the information sink in. "It's about time the animals came to my rescue." He scrunched up his face and gave me a look of genuine concern. I'm sure he went back to the station and had a long laugh with his pals: "And then, boys, do you know what she said? I bet she calls herself Mrs. Doolittle, too."

But after what I'd been through with all the animals in my house and on my property, my comment was only significant to me. The animals no longer seemed to be a burden, and I stopped flinching at their evening bouts of arguing; it was as though they became active members of my household. I needed them as much as they needed me.

I no longer view the wild animals on my farm as pests. I've actually learned to coexist with them. No matter how much they irritate me, unless they threaten my existence, or the land's existence, I've learned how to share my surroundings with them. My macho classmate was certainly right in his interpretation of animal life on the farm: If I killed animals I would have to suffer the consequences—a month of dead-animal stench in my kitchen and an imbalance of the ecosystem that would force the other animals to go elsewhere. I also believe that the animal excrement could help make my soil healthier by providing the necessary bacteria and microorganisms needed to decompose nutrients within my soil— nutrients that my grapevines can use. And besides, there is nothing more thrilling than owning a piece of land where you can observe a coyote stalking a group of deer, or watch a mountain lion strut past the front door on its way to drink out of your bird bath, or lock eyes with a live wild turkey headed for your kitchen. The truth? I understand now that country living is not without its animal adventures, and not for the faint of heart.

NON-IMPAIRING PEST CONTROLS

Other small pests common to grape-growers—mice, gophers, ground squirrels, and rabbits—can be dealt with without using poisons, nets, cages, or rifles. The easiest way to determine what type of animal is jeopardizing the vines is to assess whether the damage is coming from aboveground or below ground. The goal is to find ways to deal with the pests that don't drastically impair their livelihood or yours, and find solutions that are safe for you, and your land.

Birds

The simplest solution for controlling birds is to provide a place where they want to build nests, such as debris piles, large areas of brush, and areas with lots of hedges and trees nearby, away from your grapes. Or purchase bird netting—lots of bird netting—and cover the vines during the ripening time on up to harvest time. Repellents, noisemakers, and traps can also work. Larger vineyards often use silver metallic strips tied to the vines, scattered throughout the vineyard, that encourage extra reflections from the sun and scare the birds away.

Field Mice

Field mice can be very destructive. We all hate to admit it but they exist in abundance, whether in our homes (they chewed up my dining room table) or outdoors. Left to proliferate they can be very dangerous for the vines. Field mice feed on the bark and roots of grapevines. If you keep the area around the vines clear of weeds, ground covers, and heavy vegetation, you can control them. Fencing and vine shelters made from milk cartons also keep mice away from the base of the vines. Fortunately, there are many natural predators that find field mice very appealing: hawks, owls, cats, and even dogs.

Gophers

Vine injury at the base of the vine, and several inches beneath it in the soil, is usually caused by gophers. Gophers chew on the roots and bark of the vine, stressing it, and because gopher damage can easily go undetected, it is important to pay attention. Gophers will create earth mounds and damage irrigation lines by chewing through the hoses in search of water.

Since my pest-control strategy is to find the means that is both cost-effective and socially acceptable, a good approach to a gopher problem is to flood them out of their underground burrows and force them to seek refuge elsewhere. And if you add some fish emulsion to the water they will evacuate even sooner. Life in a swamp is not the ideal place for gophers to breed, eat, or seek shelter, so this technique should work. But it requires a huge increase in the use of scarce water. Temporarily, though, it may be an easy solution and could prove to be a very good solution for a back-yard grape-grower. Also, barn owls love to eat gophers, so if you can find one, go ahead.

Ground Squirrels and Rabbits

The culprits that cause vine injury that occurs aboveground are a little trickier to identify. Ground squirrels and rabbits feed on the fruit and foliage and chew on the bark of the vines. They can cause damage to the vine itself, as well as the fruit crop. The main difference between these two pests is that ground squirrels live underground in tunnel systems they have created, normally on the perimeter of the vineyard, and rabbits live aboveground in the brush. Both animals are very destructive to the vine. I have had an enormous problem with ground squirrels. I am embarrassed to say that since these creatures looked so scrawny, I assumed they were some form of a rat with a bushy tail. I named them squirrel-rats and later learned there was no such thing.

Once again, I reviewed my options for controlling these populations. I could hope for more of their predators: Eagles, dogs, and coyotes eat both ground squirrels and rabbits; Hawks, gopher snakes, and rattlesnakes eat ground squirrels. Low fences around the vines, or vine shelters made from milk cartons, can be used to protect the base of the vines from both pests. Of course, backyard grape-growers will not be able to rely on eagles or coyotes, but put your dog to work or buy some gopher snakes—and you might be lucky enough to get a visiting hawk to do the work.

Another way to approach any animal that is attacking your grapevine weeds is to distract them; divert them away from the grapevines by giving them another better environment for breeding, another better food source, or another better place for shelter, or as my grandfather did, drop something that is organic, smelly, and hot—like pepper mixed with flour—in their pathway. Granted, this may take some time, but no one said that keeping animals happy is an easy job (just ask any zoo keeper).

SIX

PLANT RIGHT, DON'T LET THE BAD BUGS BITE

*S*igns posted on trees around my lush winter roadsides with captions that read: "Have You Seen This Goat?" (with a hand drawn picture of a handsome billy goat) or "Pet Cat Shot" (with a sad-looking black and white photo of a Persian feline) are commonplace. Glen Ellen townspeople aren't shy about posting inquiries about such matters; they are very conscientious about their animals. The rules about posting creative signs in pursuit of lost animals or disgruntled opinions on animal abuse are acceptable and understood. Just like the concern that was generated over the lost steer on our property, a runaway goat or a bullet-struck cat are serious issues to contend with. In some cases they are the livelihood of their owners and in others they are merely adored pets.

I've become used to this world where livestock and country animals, wild or otherwise, are second in line to ourselves. In the country a dog sometimes replaces friends and horseback riding sometimes replaces team sports. We've also found that where we live there are a different set of rules to follow when it comes to getting work done around the home before winter arrives. This means monitoring levels in water tanks, determining well outputs, checking propane levels, and looking for septic line breaks by the end of fall, because no one in their right mind wants to bang around on the muddy hillside during the dreary days of winter looking for smelly septic leaks, the cause of diminishing water, or broken gas lines spewing fumes that destroy the fresh air and preclude the working mechanisms of stoves, ovens, and heating systems.

"What could be so difficult about fixing a darn gas line in our heating system?" I asked Chuck as he was on his way out the door one freezing winter when the furnace stopped. I'd neglected to check the propane meter that fall. The propane had leaked out of the line, the meter reading had dropped without my seeing it, and before I knew it we were without any comfort in our home. Rachel and I tromped through the acres of frozen ground looking for the place where the leak had occurred.

"I've found it," I yelled, digging through layers of brown goop that had previously been remnants of our dry, fertile soil. "At least we've found the problem and when the repairman gets here he can go right to the source."

We ended up waiting five long days and nights, with extra clothes and warm blankets wrapped around our freezing bodies, for that repairman. On the third day I took charge and called him again. Besides no heat, we had no hot water and no stove.

"Look," I said, seeing a reflection of my image—ripped flannel shirt, pants that were sloppy and ill-fitted, rubber boots that hit me above the knee (men's fishing waders), and red woolen gloves with the fingers cut out—in a nearby mirror, "we're all starting to turn into popsicles around here." I knew he was busy, and I was beginning to understand that country living does bring certain elements of isolation that I never spent much time thinking about in my ardent desire to get away from city life. We don't automatically have water, gas, sewer, and TV, for instance. There is no public utility company to call for quick response to any of these things should they simply cease functioning.

"My daughter Joy will bake some chocolate chip cookies for you if you can bring yourself to bump us up to the top of the list and get out here immediately," I said, trying to sound like we'd all have a good time. Grace and Dude winked at me as I made this statement, knowing that this was a complete lie because Joy was only four years old at the time and certainly not capable of making cookies yet. We all just accepted that the mere thought of baking cookies was a glorious excuse to use the oven, no matter which kid did the actual job because it meant we could all stand around with the large electric appliance wide open and get warm. We all relished the thought. "Besides," I told Grace and Dude later, "the repairman doesn't know how old Joy is." The cookies, however, must not have been tempting enough for that repairman and we waited two more days.

Everyone had their issues. "Mom," Grace said, in her practical ten-year-old tone, "I'm having nightmares about skating on a pond in the middle of the forest and falling through ice into the freezing cold water and I can't move my legs because they are so cold." She was always thinking about water.

Dude was digging through his tool box trying to devise a way to repair the broken pipe.

"I appreciate your help," I told him, "but I think we'll pass on your expertise," reminding myself that a seven-year-old was not qualified for this job. The last pipe he'd attempted to fix had turned into a giant problem when he stuck a female connection into a female connection with glue that held it just tightly enough so we couldn't get it apart and fix it correctly—male to female—without sawing it. Rachel and I had taken turns sawing the pipe, cussing our way through layers of metal.

The kids had all developed certain patterns for dealing with the unpredictability and disruption of our daily country routines. It was as if they'd each created a predictable genre for their responses to unpleasant situations. Dude was always calmly trying to figure out how to fix broken things, Grace was concerned with the horrors that a bad situation could cause, and Joy wanted to create a beautiful meal that would make everyone forget their problems.

A dog sometimes replaces friends, and that winter, when we all became edgy because we were freezing and there was no possibility of spending time outdoors in the warm sun, our dog Roofus (the dog we had after Sha-na-na and just before Bubba arrived) was a good companion who snuggled with us and made us warm. He also kept my children's spirits high, even when they missed the conveniences of the city and the cul-de-sac life of the suburbs.

On our third evening without heat, Roofus contracted a terrible cough. He had been tromping around the fields, and I thought he must have caught the dog's version of the same cough we had been suffering when the heat hadn't been working.

To my great dismay, Roofus fled into the vineyard later that evening—into the freezing cold. I ran after him, only to witness him flop down into the mud, eyes glazed over. After an unsuccessful attempt to lure him back to the house, I finally hoisted him onto the red wagon my children used to fly down the hillsides during the summer (when I wasn't looking) and wheeled him back up to the house.

I left him to get some sleep and hoped he would feel better in the morning, but when I got to the place I had laid him down early the next morning, his bed was empty. With a sliver of hope that he was maybe up to some mischief, I searched around only to find him lying by the front door in a lifeless heap. There are no manuals on coping with such things and rather than create a huge scene in front of the kids, I decided to cover the dog with a blanket and close the door to the room where he lay. It's the Scarlett O'Hara approach—not a liberated path I know—but one that affords its user lots of leeway for denial, procrastination, and optimism. Rachel and I removed him after the kids left for school. We gesticulated around the animal, shrugging our shoulders and sighing, shaking our heads in disbelief at what had happened. Hours seemed to go by before we were able to find a solution that would work for both of us. Physics work best in times like these and we attempted the physics of propulsion in order to hoist him into the back of my car. It's nothing I'm proud of, mind you. We managed, though, and my beloved pet was removed and taken to a better place—the crematorium. Had I been rational at the time, I would have considered the possibility of burying him somewhere among the oak trees and rolling hills of my twenty-four acres of property. The thought did not occur to me during my time of despair.

That night, over an open fire we built in our backyard because we still had no electricity, I made our favorite stew with meat that was given to us from a close friend who raised beef cattle. I normally would flambé the beef in cognac and simmer it for hours in home-made broth and a splash of my favorite Ravenswood Zinfandel, with fresh carrots, potatoes, and bay leaves from our garden. That night we stuck to tradition, though, and sat around smelling the delicious fumes from the boiling hot food, soaking our tears in our grief over the loss of our pet. The smell of the savory soup, as we sipped away on the Ravenswood wine, lifted our spirits and gave me the strength to remember better times. I recalled the early days right after we'd bought our property, and a point when I needed to find a winery to buy my grapes. One of the places I went and later ended up selling my fruit to was Ravenswood Winery, where I met Joel Peterson and Reed Foster, the boys whose winery slogan reads "No Wimpy Wines." We sat in Joel's office, a rustic wooden cabin tucked behind the winery, and I learned about some of the healthy philosophies of Ravenswood. That was ten years ago, before the winery became one of the biggest in the country, and I was impressed by their friendly, down-to-earth approaches concerning sustainable farming, great wine, and how to run a harmonious business. They haven't changed over the years. That night, despite the loss of Roofus, the taste of the soup on my tongue interspersed with sips of Ravenswood reminded me of those good times and brought back happy thoughts of all the winter nights we'd spent with Roofus curled up at our feet while we ate stew and drank Ravenswood wine.

The autopsy showed that Roofus had been poisoned, probably from hunting and eating an animal that had ingested warfarin, the poison of choice for controlling the rodent population. *How could I have let this happen—again?* I chided myself.

It took me a while to get over his death. I was upset for days, and although my family didn't blame me for Roofus's death, I still felt directly responsible. Why was I still paying the price for my past mistakes and the previous mismanagement of my farmland? I was no longer using poisons, pesticides, or any chemicals, so it must have been left over; it must have remained in the soil, or the roots of the vines. This trauma further deepened my convictions about the use of harmful products on my land. It reconfirmed my perspective on how I must view the larger animals roaming around my property, and it changed my outlook on smaller insect "pests." I clearly understood the importance of letting the larger animals maintain an uninterrupted food chain, and this understanding soon filtered down to how I felt about the insects in my vineyard.

I now approach these perceived nuisances without destroying the ecological community. The common theme with insects is that maintaining a balance is the best way to continue the health and quality of soil. By wiping one pest completely out I destroy both the pest and the predator that needs that pest to survive. A giant "hole," one that is injurious to a farm or garden, is created within the environment when one element is destroyed. I've figured out which insects frequent the territory of grapevines, what they look like, how I can deal with them ethically, and how the natural food chain can aide in this process. By identifying insects and knowing that there are alternatives to controlling them, other than poisons, they don't seem as intimidating and threatening, and besides, watching them can be a great pastime and a unique hobby.

I've also learned that all of these insects become less detrimental to my plants when the grapevines and their soil are healthy. There is no scientific proof of this; however, there is evidence in my own vineyard, and the vineyards of others, to confirm the belief that a sickly plant becomes healthier when it is grown in healthy soil that is full of living organisms.

When the human body becomes ill, one takes medicines that kill the illness (and sometimes the body). An antibiotic may wipe out the illness but it may also wipe out other things that are needed in order for the person to remain healthy. Translate this to farming and gardening: Over the past fifty years when a plant becomes ill, we've sprayed pesticides, herbicides, and insecticides to kill the disease, insect, or unwanted weed (and sometimes the plant). The issue then becomes: How do we maintain our immune system so that we do not become ill? How do we sustain our plants' health so that they stay strong and able to fend off diseases and pests? By monitoring the vines to figure out, based on the damage, whether the insects are posing a real threat or whether they are providing a healthier environment, I have consistently determined the latter. And if I plant right, placing the vines in healthy soil, the bad bugs don't bite and don't penetrate the vine.

KNOW THE BUGS IN YOUR GARDEN

Insects That Feed on Buds and Baby Shoots (usually at night)

BEETLES

Grape bud beetles and grape flea beetles, aphids, and ants love to feed on the new buds and shoots of the vine, especially at night. This may pose a problem for those who don't relish the thought of traipsing through their garden at night looking for these pests (especially in late winter when it's cold). But don't worry because Mother Nature is on the grape-grower's side, and if there is no time to do a nightly garden stroll, the animal community will probably take care of the problem long before any of these pests become a threat to your vines.

GRAPE BUD BEETLES

These are small, gray-colored hopping beetles that eat the center out of the buds before budburst. Sticky traps (purchased at gardening stores) can be placed around the vines to thwart the efforts of beetles. Birds, reptiles, and certain types of mammals eat beetles.

GRAPE FLEA BEETLES

These are small, purple or bluish hopping beetles that also eat the center out of the buds before budburst. As with the grape bud beetle, sticky traps, birds, reptiles, and other mammals help destroy this insect.

APHIDS

These are oval-shaped soft insects that are generally brown when found on the vine. Spraying the grapevine leaves with a soapy mixture (½ gallon water with ¼ cup biodegradable liquid soap) or fresh water will kill aphids and not harm the vines. My grandfather used to puree oranges and spray the liquid from the mixture in his garden to kill aphids. Ladybugs, frogs, toads, and birds consume large amounts of aphids.

ANTS

These are small, black insects with round heads and corrugated bodies. A solution of equal parts sugar and borax will kill ants. If you have an abundance of ants, then you probably have a multitude of aphids because ants like to feed off the excrement of aphids.

* * *

Insects That Feed on Leaves

SPIDER MITES

Willamette (Western), Twospotted (Western), European Red (Eastern), and Pacific (Western) Grape Leaf Hoppers and Western Grape Leaf Skeletonizers eat the new leaves on the shoots of the vines.

MITES

The Willamette and Pacific mites are yellow with black spots; the European mite is red. They are tiny insects with eight legs. Mites deposit a thick dusty remnant on the underside of the leaf, where they deposit their eggs. The leaves sometimes turn yellow or red and become small and curled. If the leaves start to curl and change color (early in the season) use treatments of sulfur dust. Other mites, the sixspotted thrip and the ladybird beetle, feed on these mites.

GRAPE LEAF HOPPERS

These are thin insects that are mostly yellow with speckles of red and brown. Leaf hoppers attach themselves to the leaves and puncture them leaving a white spot that damages the leaves. A soap solution (½ gallon water with ¼ cup biodegradable liquid soap) will remove them. The pirate bug, ladybird beetle, green and brown lacewing, and the Anagrus, a parasitic wasp, eat the grape leaf hopper.

WESTERN GRAPE LEAF SKELETONIZERS

These insects are easy to spot in their final stage: yellow, purple, and black striped caterpillars. They eat away at the entire leaf. Pick them off with your hand. The Ametadoria misella, a parasitic fly, and Apanteles harrisinae, a parasitic wasp and a virus that attacks the gut of the larvae, naturally control this pest.

* * *

Insects That Eat Grapes

ORANGE TORTRIX MOTHS

These are light brown moths that cause fruit rot by puncturing the grapes and allowing bacteria and fungus to enter the berry. Wasps feed on the larvae; spiders, green lacewings, and pirate bugs also consume the moths.

THRIPS

These pests have wings, skinny bodies, and they can fly and jump. They feed on the grapes leaving a scarred patch on the fruit. A soap solution (½ gallon water with ½ cup biodegradable liquid soap) will remove them. The green lacewing, ladybird beetles, and the Anagrus, a parasitic wasp, eat thrips.

MEALYBUGS

These are white and soft looking with an oval body. They cause contamination of the grapes by laying their eggs and leaving a white, sticky clump that looks like dust. Grapegrowers can remove them by wiping the berries clean with a damp cloth. There are many natural predators: pirate bugs, beetles, brown lacewings, and spiders. Watch for ants, though, because they inhibit these other predators. If the ants are too prevalent near the grapes, provide them (the ants) with another host, boil them, or cover them in chocolate—whatever it takes to get rid of them.

SEVEN

DON'T COUNT YOUR GRAPES
BEFORE THEY RIPEN

*M*y love of lavender has caused problems in my marriage. Chuck says it smells like a medicinal anodyne that should be used on horses. "It probably is used on horses," I say, "and I think it's a versatile, astounding plant that I can't live without."

Chuck has told me that his greatest fear in life is to die without having accomplished anything, and mine is that I will die having accomplished so much that I was never able to stop long enough to soak up the beauty of life.

"I need my lavender," I say, "it helps me stay calm and slow down."

"That's ridiculous," he says. But I think lavender scares him. Needless to say, many years ago I bought twenty-five tiny English lavender plants and stuck them into my garden. They are now each four-feet wide and three-feet tall.

"What's that lavender-colored flower on the chicken?" Chuck snapped one night at dinner.

"Oh that, that's the pretty purple edible flower from that special chive I'm growing," I respond, staying calm. He doesn't question me anymore about why many of our meals have purple things floating in them because I've figured out many other flowers that can serve as an alias for lavender; and maybe he's realized it's just a waste of time for him to ask anymore.

Because I'm unable to control the lavender's vigor, we have lavender tea, lavender ice cream, lavender sauces, lavender soap, lavender bread, lavender-stuffed pillows, and lavender oil. Besides Chuck, only Bubba seems to mind, because he sneezes and shakes when I spritz him with lavender water. Chuck doesn't take much notice except when winter rolls around; he can't escape the smell any longer since the weather is bad, the doors are all closed, and he has no place to go to get away from the lavender that is stored in tin buckets, pillows, and bags throughout our tightly shut house. Some lavender-growers don't have flowers in the winter, but if taken care of properly I can harvest a second crop that comes late summer and by the time it's picked, hung upside down for two weeks, and the oil falls down the stem and into the flower, we are inundated with winter lavender.

Other than fighting over the lavender, the twinkle of a California wine country winter is blissful and calming. Sonoma County natives take more care in creating exotic meals, since there is less time spent outdoors, and their food gardens turn from corn, tomatoes, green beans, blueberries, raspberries, and strawberries to arugula, cilantro, carrots, broccoli, chives, and mixed winter lettuces like valeria, red butterworth, vulcan, rouge d'hiver, brunia, and romaine. Arugula and brunia with red onions, winter pears, and freshly grated Italian parmesan in a citrus vinaigrette, roasted chicken with lemon juice and rosemary, and pureed carrots with creamy butter and cracked pepper disseminate smells throughout my kitchen. And the wine—always abundant—shifts my notice to reds, from Cabernets, to Merlots, to Zinfandels, to Meritages. It's just the best time of year to fill your stomach, drink some red wine, and hibernate.

Sometimes I take for granted the impact winter hibernation impresses on humans, animals, and plants—as the natural resources become depleted or dormant. Although humans don't technically hibernate, and they don't suffer from lack of food around here, animals can suffer from not finding their share of food during droughts, or even extremely damp winters.

One winter, a bear—searching for large amounts of fish—ended up frighteningly close to my house. He chose, instead, a wonderful inn just down the road in the town of Glen Ellen. The bear should have been building a comfortable den for his winter hibernation; however, he was ungraciously digging through garbage cans and scaring residents because he hadn't stocked up on enough food for his winter hibernation. (I should have invited him to scoop up ants from my vineyard.) Not being able to tell the difference between a pond and a pool, he ended up diving (reported by two swimming New York tourists) into the pool at the lodge. The New Yorkers scattered and the bear, scared by all the to-do, splashed around briefly—likely looking for fish—and then climbed a big tree next to the pool. He hung out there for quite some time.

Rachel, the kids, and I arrived when the police were preparing to shoot the bear with a tranquilizer gun. They were successful, and once he was sedated it took hours to get him loaded on the stretcher while he clung to the tree branch with all four appendages, his engorged belly swinging below the limb looking like an acrobat who slips from his tightrope and suspends precariously from the wire. There were firemen, police, and a multitude of ladders placed around the base of the tree as the departments worked together to navigate the heavy stretcher down to the ground. We later found out that they drove the bear to a remote area and dropped him off (once he awoke from the sedation), hoping he would settle down, find a comfortable nest, and lapse into a long sleep.

We had just arrived home from the bear experience and were whipping up some toasted pumpkin seeds and Mexican hot chocolate for a snack when a friendly skunk wandered onto our property.

"That skunk's not friendly," Rachel complained. "There's no such thing as a friendly skunk wandering around during the day—when he should be sleeping."

"I think he is; otherwise why would he come up to us and not turn his backside, and stomp his feet like he's going to spray," I said. It was the first time we'd ever disagreed about how to proceed with taking care of a problem on the property. At her insistence, I called up the local veterinarian to find out how to handle this animal. "Should I cage him?" I inquired.

"Nope." he said, matter-of-factly. "You need to feed him during the day. He is not getting enough nourishment at night, the foodstuffs are low, and he is still looking for food once the day begins. When his appetite is satisfied, he will go back to being active at night and sleeping during the day."

"Feed him?" I grimaced. That never entered my mind.

I probably should have caged him, because shortly thereafter, I invited several girlfriends and their children over for a relaxing afternoon. We decided to build big, beautiful wreaths for a fundraiser at our children's school. The skunk was the farthest thing from my mind as we pieced together the wreaths and designed creative patterns. I should have warned the group that there was a "harmless" skunk on the property and that he was just looking for something to eat, but it was too late. The kids began chasing him; the adults recognized this as a potentially dangerous situation and started running after their kids.

The skunk responded by streaking through a field full of dormant oak trees and twigs of various shapes and sizes. My voice could be heard echoing throughout the property, "It's okay! Leave him alone!"

Worse than the actual event was the day after. All of the adults—myself included—were covered with poison oak. "What the hell?" Chuck protested. "I thought you promised to store the lavender in the garage for the winter." The house was extremely fragrant with the smell of lavender since we had all rubbed and sprayed it on our poison oak.

"I did store it in the garage," I retorted, scratching my chest. "The problem is that we're all wearing it." Little did we know that you should avoid walking through oak fields in winter, no matter how barren the ground looks, because those dried-up "sticks" are not completely harmless. As witnessed by our outbreak and weeks of scratching that followed, they're very much alive and capable of infecting you with their poisonous oil.

✳ ✳ ✳

Just like poison oak, grapevines appear lifeless and dead in winter; however, they are merely taking a long, bear-like nap in preparation for the explosion that will occur in the spring. Similar to a grizzly bear sleeping in a quiescent state, winter grapevines should not be underestimated. In winter, dormancy is an integral part of the life cycle of both bears and grapevines. Like a fall bear preparing for its spring awakening by consuming huge amounts of fish before its winter slumber, a fall grapevine lays the foundation for its spring renewal by soaking up large volumes of nutrients before its winter dormancy. And during their winter snooze, even though the bear and the vine look spiritless and dead, they are completely alive—as is poison oak!

Even though many grape farmers would rather hibernate with the bears, winter is the season to labor over the future of the crop by putting in some long hours of pruning handicraft. And there is only one efficient way I know of for grape-growers to prune their vines. It includes grabbing a pair of pruning shears, a sweater, and a hat, and heading out into the cold to wack off the extra parts of the vine that won't be needed for the next growing season. You'll notice that in my list of accessories I didn't mention a pair of gloves. I used to wear gloves for pruning vines, but I received such hassle from my classmates, that I ultimately learned to grin and bear it and prune without gloves.

I learned everything I care to know about pruning when I was enrolled in viticulture classes. As we stood in class, which consisted of many acres of vineyard, my cold hands ached (which is why I wore gloves) and my feet were numb from the chilling winds that blew through the valley. In a tactful way, my professor suggested that engaging in hand exercises—squeezing a rubber ball over and over—might be a good way to spend my evenings and greatly improve my pruning expertise. For me, the kind suggestion stirred up thoughts about tractor class and my need to catch up with the rest of the students. Even after strengthening my hands to meet the requirements of successful pruning, I struggled against my feelings of inadequacy—which is why I don't wear the gloves anymore, even when there's no one around to hassle me.

Pruning wasn't all bad while I was in school, though, because on many of those frosty winter days that we spent tromping through various vineyards in Sonoma County learning about different training styles, we were almost always greeted by the winery owners, and in their appreciation of our education, and their desire to warm us up, served some of their best wines. Preston Vineyards in Dry Creek Valley was especially eye-opening for me, and I was introduced to a wave of grape-growers and winemakers that called themselves the Rhone Rangers. Up until that point it seemed to me that most of the wineries were making wines like Chardonnay, Sauvignon Blanc, Cabernet Sauvignon, Pinot Noir, Zinfandel, and Merlot, but alas there was a winery that was making Rhone-style wines in California. An appetite for Rhone varietals, and the belief that our area was perfect for growing Rhone grapes like Syrah, Grenache, Cinsault, Mourvedre, Carignane, Marsanne, Roussanne, and Viognier, led Lou and Susan Preston to begin growing and making wine from these traditional French Côte du Rhone varietals—in California. They were with the movement that had started in the early 1970s that believed these grapes were well-suited to our California climate, that they produced fine wines with elegant flavor profiles, and that they had aromatics that paired well with food.

I had a deep affection for the Rhone varietals since I'd spent a year abroad when I was twenty as a foreign exchange student studying art and literature in Avignon, France. The Côte du Rhone region wines were served in place of water to the natives living in Provence, and the family I lived with would take their empty jugs to the back alleys in Avignon, where large tanks of wine were hidden away in concrete floored, ancient rooms, and fill them up for just five francs. And while on break from classes, my girlfriend Kirsten and I used to load up our backpacks, grab our bikes, and ride to Chateauneuf-du-Pape—the illustrious red wine region in the Côte du Rhone appellation—to picnic, drink wine, and lay in the vineyards. As we picnicked in the vineyards, our bellies full from wine, cheese, and paté, we fantasized about how our lives would be if we married one of those famous French winemakers. Our dreams didn't manifest— at least not those dreams. But without really knowing it, I became very attached to the Rhone-style wines and also to the traditional head-trained style that I remembered from France. Once I began studying viticulture I could never understand why the Americans had abandoned the rustic training style.

Like most gardening procedures, pruning is done many different ways and with many differences of opinion. Pruning allows growers the opportunity to create a balanced plant that produces quality fruit and is technically sound. Our community has a yearly competition held at the end of January called the Sonoma Valley Pruning Contest that judges these characteristics: technical and artistic. This is a major event that receives local publicity and creates excitement among the valley farm workers. It is a great honor for those who win. Contestants' pruning abilities are judged based on the excellence of their cuts, the finished shape (visual quality, buds left, length of spurs), and the time it takes to complete. Winners move on to a countywide competition and then a regional championship. In the process, pruners develop aesthetically pleasing artistic shapes that aren't always learned from study and technical prowess, but are instead an intuitive talent.

In my opinion, there is no grapevine more beautiful than the ancient French Rhone vines with their gnarly trunks and distorted figures that lend the viewer hundreds of years of history—both tragic and jubilant. They are scattered throughout fields, beckoning travelers with their charming allure and wise demeanor. Like a palm reader who foretells the future, these vines disclose the past; it's written all over their façade in all the knotty partitions of their years. They tell the story of many seasons among the vines: families picnicking under the fall shelter of their turning leaves, wartime troops staggering across their frozen winter soil, children floating carelessly under their extending springtime shoots, and summer lovers passionately sucking away on their intoxicating berries. This system is uncomplicated, beautifully simplistic, and magical; it's the opposite of opulence and the antitheses of greed.

ISSUES TO CONSIDER
FOR A TRIUMPHANT WINTER FORMULA

How can a grape-grower produce large quantities of grapes (high quality, of course) for winemaking using different spacing, training, and pruning procedures? The best approach is one that is cost-effective, time efficient, and beautifies the land. Remember, too, that grapevines are always happy spreading freely in the direction of the sun and climbing their way around whatever they come in contact with.

Spacing, Planting New Grapevines, Training, and Pruning

SPACING

Spacing—how far apart the vines are planted—is somewhat controversial. Ten years ago the adopted spacing style for American grape-growers, vines planted 6 feet apart with a 10-foot space between the rows, was believed to produce the highest tonnages and best fruit quality, and be the most cost-effective for manual labor, tractor usage, fertilizer, pesticide, and insecticide consumption. Things have changed. Manual labor costs are different; smaller European tractors are available; and farmers are using less chemicals and more organics. Some farmers remain happy with the style of ten years ago, while others choose to plant their vines 3 feet apart or less. They believe this increases the grape yield per acre, ensures heavier crops in the first few years, and provides an overall increase in fruit quality. Your concerns certainly encompass these topics, but they lie elsewhere as well: available area in your yard and finding a suitable fence, arbor, or wall with the highest amount of sunlight. (Spacing the vines less than three feet apart can sometimes promote nutrient competition because the plants roots may be too close together; however, if you keep your soils healthy this too can be managed.)

After you decide on your spacing requirements and plop your new vines into the ground, no matter how you decide to train or prune your vines, the winter procedures for new grapevines will be the same for all regions and varieties for the first two years. The goal for these first two years is to develop a strong, healthy root system and to gain sturdy, vertical growth from one of the shoots. Although you may be anxious to produce grapes early on, don't be tempted to count your chickens before they hatch, because in the first two years it is best to concentrate the energy on the vegetative growth of the vines. Once the vines reach their intended height, you can shift the goal to producing the biggest and best crop. New grapevines will consist of a rootstock and a grape variety (Merlot, Chardonnay, etc.) grafted onto the rootstock. They will generally be one-year-old dormants, two-year-old dormants, or potted vines. In warmer regions they can be planted anywhere from March to April, and in cooler regions anywhere from May to June.

✳ ✳ ✳

Planting New Grapevines

Three-Year Procedure for New Grapevines

INITIAL PLANTING IN SPRING

1. Dig a 2-foot-deep hole

2. Trim the roots 6–8 inches at the bottom (creates hormonal stimulation that encourages rapid growth)

3. Place vine in hole (remove buds below soil surface; graft union needs to be 4 inches above soil)

4. Cut top back leaving 2–3 buds

5. Mound soil over top of vine (about 10 inches covering graft union and buds)

6. After one month, remove mound and replace with ½-gallon milk/juice cartons

7. Keep soil moist for 6 weeks

8. After 6 weeks and for next 2 years, water with 5 gallons of water per week (rainfall included)

FIRST WINTER FOLLOWING PLANTING

1. Cut vine back to one cane and leave 2 buds (green shoots are now brown and called canes)

2. For free-standing vines, drive wooden stake (height based on final height of vine) into ground a couple of inches from the vine

3. After spring growth (when shoots reach 15–18 inches) remove buds and shoots that are not in upward growth position (leaving one single shoot with leaves)

4. Tie shoot to stake, fence, or arbor

SECOND WINTER FOLLOWING PLANTING

1. Cut cane back to intended height

2. Tie cane to stake

3. Leave 6 buds at top of cane and remove all other buds or, if diameter of cane is less than 5/16 inch, cut vine back to 2 buds (some vines may need this and others may not)

Training

Training a vine refers to the permanent shape the gardener is seeking to produce. The way you train your vines ultimately depends upon whether they will be free standing (for those with more space and no fence structures), climbing an arbor (coverings or walkways), or spreading over a fence or wall (already existing in backyard). The grower needs to make this determination and encourage the vine to grow either vertically or horizontally, depending upon the final shape needed. (Note: The higher the vine must grow, the more years it will take.) Backyard grape-growers need not construct complicated, expensive trellis systems that require countless hours of fabrication and needless headaches. (I've done this and it's not fun.)

For free-standing vines—or vines using arbors as support—I like a training system that requires no trellis other than a simple wooden stake. The system is called head-training because the vine takes on the appearance of a large head perched atop a trunk. Grapevines naturally take on this shape after the second year of pruning by ending up with a single trunk, and new wood arising from the buds on their top half. For those who are unfamiliar with this system, just picture a standard California or Florida palm tree that is anywhere from 1–3 feet tall. I like to use this analogy because palm leaves extend from a single trunk and look like an elaborate head-dress resting on a thin body. Head-trained vines look similar. With the head-trained system, backyard growers can use either spur pruning and cane pruning.

Free-Standing (or Arbors): Head-Trained System After Third Year

1. Standard height of vine will be 18–36 inches (cooler regions should be higher off ground away from cold air)

2. The vines can be trained as high as 7 feet for an arbor

3. Use wooden stake for support

4. Plant with 3-foot diameter (any closer causes nutrient competition, shading to shoots and fruit)

When training the vines for a fence or wall, there is another system that is unlike the head-trained system, but works well for this type of situation. (Use the head-trained system if you prefer.) The technique is called cordon training. This system looks like a person standing upright with their arms extended out in both directions (minus the head). You'll have a trunk that grows almost to the top of your wall or fence; there will be two cordons (or arms) extended out from the top of the trunk. My vines, the phylloxera vines that were ripped out before the new vines were planted, were on this type of system. It's a good system that's reliable and easy to manage, and is used by many commercial grape-growers. This type of training can be used with either spur pruning or cane pruning, depending upon the vigor of your vines.

Fence or Wall: Cordon Trained Vine After Third Year

1. Standard height of vine will be 4–8 feet

2. During the second summer, top off vine and choose 2 laterals (one on each side of trunk and 5–12 inches below the top of vine)

3. Tie laterals horizontally to top of fence or wall

4. During the second winter, prune lateral/cordon leaving 2 feet of length (if cordons are less than $\frac{1}{16}$ inch in diameter, cut them back and wait for stronger canes next year)

Pruning

Pruning the vine refers to removing parts of the vine on a yearly basis in order to determine how many buds will be left at the start of each new season. The continued growth of a vine without pruning, year after year, may land you a plant that becomes larger than your house. And if your grapevines are not pruned, they will become a complex tangle of parts that produce too much fruit of very low quality. Pruning is done to remove the expendable portions of the vine—canes, shoots, and leaves—in order to stimulate spring growth, improve the shape of the vine, balance production, and yield high-quality fruit.

The pruning cuts should be made with sharp tools to avoid splitting the wood, which creates more wounding to the vine. I use both hands and it helps me make a cleaner, sharper cut. When canes are pruned for spurs, cut at a slight angle approximately 1/2 inch above the bud. Because of the angle, the top cut will be around 2 inches above the bud. If the cut is made too far above the bud, in between the internode, the pith will be exposed and this can later allow mold growth that can destroy the bud below. When cutting off a cane or spur completely, place the blade of your pruning tool against the grapevine and cut at an angle upwards as close to the vine as possible. Any stub can hinder the healing process of this type of cut, as well as mess up the look of your vine.

I would sooner give you verbal descriptions of certain pruning procedures and let you create your own finished piece (the finished vine should be like a piece of art—a product of individual creativity) rather than show you a picture of how these grapevines should look. Those darn weeds just don't look the way they look in the textbook pictures. Your biggest job in winter, then—with or without a textbook—is to prune the vines back every year so they don't swallow up your yard and climb their way around the exterior, and maybe even interior, of your house. (Forget about taking a break from life—as the bears do—because when it comes to grape-growing, winter is not the season to rest.)

Which Month Should I Prune My Grapevines?

The time of pruning depends upon the weather in your region; however, no matter where you live, definitely don't prune the vines before the leaves drop. (Pruning before the leaves drop can stop the vines ability to accumulate nutritional reserves for spring growth.) Pruning in December will promote the vigor of shoot growth (more vegetative development) and cause an earlier bud break by two to three weeks, and pruning in late March or early April will lower the vigor of the vine and increase the fruit crop. The vine cannot have energy for heavy vegetative growth and a heavy crop, so pick the objective. By accelerating bud break with earlier pruning, there is an increased risk to the productivity of the vine if the weather gets cold and rainy. In warmer regions this won't be a factor. Just make sure the pruning is done before the buds burst (the average daily temperature gets above 50 degrees Fahrenheit) or immediately after they rupture.

Free-Standing Head-Trained System with Spur Pruning (full maturity vine should have 14–28 buds left)

1. Prune canes, the permanent arms left after harvest (leaving 5-7 pruned fruiting canes called spurs)

2. Cut fruiting canes into spurs with 2, 3, or 4 buds (depending upon vigor of vine)

3. Fruiting canes/spurs should be anywhere from 6-8 inches apart

4. During growing season, remove all growth below spurs

* Vigor of vine can be determined by looking at length of cane, before pruning and after harvest. Canes: 1 foot or less have low vigor, 3 feet have moderate vigor, and up to 10 feet have high vigor.

Free-Standing Head-Trained System with Cane Pruning (works well for tall arbor or trellis; full maturity vine should have 30–40 buds left)

1. Prune canes (leave 2–4 spur-like canes, depending upon vigor of vine)

2. Allow 8–15 buds on each spur-like cane

3. Once shoots appear on pruned spur-like canes, after bud-burst, lay them across the top of arbor or trellis

* Low vigor vines should have eight buds per spur-like cane and high vigor vines should have 15 buds per spur-like cane

Fence or Wall Cordon Trained System with Spur Pruning

1. Prune each of the 2 cordons/arms leaving anywhere from 4–7 (depends upon vigor of vine) 2-budded spurs, for California or warmer regions, and five 4-budded spurs for cooler regions (some buds may not produce shoots if too much frost occurs)

2. Four-budded vines, if all buds produced healthy shoots thin down to 2 shoots per arm

Fence or Wall Cordon System with Can Pruning

1. Prune each of the 2 cordons/arms leaving 2–4 (depends upon vigor of vine) canes with 10 buds per cane

2. At base of each cane leave a 2-budded renewal spur for the next year's fruiting cane

The common denominator in all of these pruning situations is that at full maturity the vines end up with 40–60 buds (except the head-trained spur pruned vine which may only end up with 20–30 buds). In deciding whether to spur prune or cane prune, there are a few factors to be considered: weather in your region, and vigor of your variety.

Cane pruning with renewal spurs is ideal for cooler regions like the northern and eastern areas of the United States, and is suitable for most varieties. At the base of each cane leave a 2-budded renewal spur for the next year's fruiting cane. There are more buds left on the canes after pruning (in case frost kills some of the buds). Once the canes produce their crop and at pruning time the next year, cut the previous year's fruiting cane back to a 2-budded renewal spur for the next year's crop. The last year's renewal spur's shoot, now a cane, is used for the new fruiting cane. (Each year's fruit producing canes and renewal spurs are rotated.) By leaving a renewal spur, in case the fruiting canes become damaged, you are assured a back-up system when the weather is not on your side (plan on it never being perfect). This system will require some extra work if the weather does not destroy any of your buds: shoot thinning in late spring to control heavy growth and shading, and shoot positioning in the summer to expose fruit to sun exposure (no shading) and aeration.

Spur pruning is better suited for warmer climates in the southern and western areas of the United States, and for highly vigorous vines. It is a simple pruning technique that is easily maintained, and allows good fruit exposure. The biggest disadvantage is that it takes more time to establish the permanent trunk or arms, and may produce less fruit because there are fewer buds left after pruning. (In cooler regions the loss of buds from frost may reduce crop significantly.)

Visual signs and common sense can help the gardener adapt techniques for cane and spur pruning. Make decisions on your pruning based on how healthy the vine is and how good your fruit is. For example, if you choose to cane prune and the vines are struggling—not enough buds and fruit that won't ripen—then leave less canes after the next pruning. (You are over-stressing the vine.) On the other hand, if the vines growth was vigorous, the fruit was good, then leave more canes.

The good news is that badly pruning the vines will not kill them. There really is no right way, but only accepted ways that appear to be advantageous based upon specific climate and production requirements. Although people love to expound on the "right" way to train and prune grapevines, for the backyard gardener the goal should really me more about having fun, producing a plant that looks the way you want it to, and creating a unique piece of art that gives you personal satisfaction and many hours of joy.

The grower must always think about the final shape of their vine and make adjustments long before the vine is fully matured. And they must also be aware of the injury they inflict while making the pruning cuts. Viticulturists talk about pruning wounds, a worrisome byproduct produced from making cuts on the vine. When a cut is made, the vine—just like humans—must heal its injury. This is done by the vine's internal creation of thyloses, a sticky substance that fills in the gap and stops sap from seeping through. Large wounds (over 1 inch) usually can't heal, so pruners must avoid cuts of this size by removing unwanted shoots and canes before they get too large.

Of utmost importance for some is the issue of how many great bottles of wine they ultimately want to produce, while for others it will be aesthetic and whether you want to feast your eyes on free-standing vines, or vines on fences, arbors, and walls. If you choose the former, you'll definitely need to prune.

If everything runs according to plan (it never does), assume that a highly stressed and therefore low-producing single grapevine will generate approximately 12 pounds of grapes. Since it takes 16 pounds of grapes to produce 1 gallon of wine, then 2 fully mature grapevines will give you 1 gallon of wine. The process of growing grapes and making wine should never be looked upon as an exact science because the variables that come into play can greatly impact the final results. There will be loss from less-than-favorable seasonal temperatures, pests, disease, and the winemaking process.

EIGHT

A GLASS OF WINE HEALS
ALL WOUNDS

*I*t was the end of winter when Rachel had to go back to England. I'll never forget it. Before she left we buried ourselves in the rituals of the winter months—pruning, chasing animals from the property, cleaning the farm equipment in preparation for spring—knowing full well that the day would soon come when she'd have to leave the States. She'd spent years with us, become my confidante and a member of the family, and learned the ways of the California wine country, but she had to go home to her native land and continue her life as a police detective. They wanted her back, and she'd been promoted to a high-ranking, special force group that few English women had ever achieved in Britain. I had to let her go.

In the final days before she left we spent hours in the kitchen preparing gourmet meals, chopping and dicing our pain, hiding our feelings in the tantalizing warmth of an innovative meal and the medicinal benefits of bold, red wines. Grace and Dude picked fresh greens daily and Joy washed the bugs and soil off the leaves. Mashed potatoes with essence of walnut and a drop of truffle oil, lavender and rosemary baked lamb, flash-grilled hearts of romaine with pureed anchovies and spicy garlic dressing, and roasted pine nuts and skinned grapefruit sections covered in woody olive oil and balsamic vinegar soothed our spirits and drowned our sorrow. And we drank mouth-watering wines like old vine Sangiovese from Seghesio Family Winery in the Alexander Valley of Sonoma County with its aged character and pure Italian flame, and berry-flavored Cabernet Sauvignon from Kenwood Winery that came from fruit grown on Jack London's ranch and was in a bottle with his bookplate logo of a wolf head stamped on the front. I wanted Rachel to never forget the novel about the California wine country, and I wanted her to always think of us with a smile across her face when she drank a glass of wine—even if it wasn't from Sonoma County.

It was December and community press time in Glen Ellen on the actual day that Rachel left us. We stopped to watch as the olive growers from the region cooperatively mixed their olives—Mission, Kalamata, Frantoio, to name a few—into the presses and filled their containers with the oil that ran out. I was pleased that Rachel would be leaving with one last memory of the uniqueness of Glen Ellen and the Sonoma County region. Green, red, purple, and black olives were dumped into the public bin, their colors bursting with ripeness. Cars pulling up with baskets of rich olives, and trucks dumping large amounts of olives hurriedly weighed their loads—working within the confines of the twenty-four hour time period between picking and pressing—and quickly dropped their goods into the press. Woody, peppery, mellow—no one would know from one year to the next what their olive oil would taste like because it was all dependent upon the ripeness of the combined olives. Just like a winemaker blending the juice from his different grapes to produce a new flavorful wine each year, olive oil has a special flavor that changes from one year to the next.

On our way back from the airport after dropping Rachel off, I couldn't breathe. It felt like someone had squeezed my chest so tightly that I was suffocating. I was afraid of being alone, and I felt abandoned by everyone except my children. I had come to expect that Chuck would never be home to help me on the farm, and now Rachel was gone.

The panic attacks went on until I figured out that I could survive in the country on my own. This didn't happen overnight. I had become accustomed to a certain way of life and it was gone. I was used to chatting with Rachel over our morning coffee, arguing about who had to fix the broken pipes and whose turn it was to check the vines, sipping great wine over our mistakes at the end of a hard day while we revealed the ridiculous bloopers to Chuck. Like a baby first learning to walk, I started out slowly, taking notice of every move I made, every farm chore I did reminded me I was alone. My kids knew my pain and they tried in every possible way to console me when I felt as though I couldn't breathe, like the life was being sucked out of my body. Joy made me herbal tea, Grace swam with me, and Dude fixed everything that broke around the house. I took notice of every detail of my life as one does when they are lonely. But this gave me insight into things I might have missed had I always been comfortable.

Driving through the town of Glen Ellen, past establishments like the Chauvet Hotel, the Jack London Lodge, Roseann's Haircutting, and the Garden Court Café, I noticed that buildings didn't really change with the seasons the way grapevines did. Should I keep changing with the seasons or should I remain solid like the structures in my town? I didn't know. I need to accept change and stay true to my own convictions, I told myself. I had found it so difficult to shift my views when we first moved to the country, but time had altered that. Once a caretaker of the land who had followed the guidelines of the chemical companies, I had now turned my back on their principles and looked for other ways. This was my vision, and it had come to me through acceptance of change. I had to keep thinking this way in order to go on; it gave me solace. The excitement of following change and learning new things kept me going when I felt so intensely lonely.

I got over the fact that there was no longer anyone to help me with the land; I got over the fact that I had made mistakes; I got over the fact that I felt abandoned; and I moved on. I had to. Time was on my side—it helped me heal—and also the desire to continue to understand and accept new things.

Some of my most memorable moments from that period in my life came from the times I shared with my children while driving in our car. Since Grace, Dude, and Joy all went to different schools that were thirty minutes away from our home, there was little time for me to feel lonely or sorry for myself, and our car time became an important escape. I now think of my car as a chariot. The dictionary gives chariot this definition: "An ancient horse-drawn two-wheeled vehicle used in war, races, and processions; a light four-wheeled carriage used for ceremonial occasions or for pleasure." Since I take the liberty of analyzing every detail of my life, I've decided that the life we share in our vehicle—the pleasurable imagery we construe, the speeds we travel, the races we run, and the fights we engage in—certainly places it in another category beyond transportation alone. We aren't driving around in an ancient horse-drawn vehicle, but referring to our car as a chariot was our symbolic substitute, and a poetic synonym that accurately described our most frequented alternate living quarters.

We became poets in the car; stories were embellished—to a captive audience with no escape—and opinions were expressed using language that was both lyrical and melodramatic. The epics that ensued—vivid descriptions that produced exquisite, mental images—were not to be taken lightly because this was where we grew together, the space where our spiritual minds resided. Our car was a pleasurable shelter, a place where we took care of each other's emotional needs and learned to watch and understand change.

Our little town of Glen Ellen had gone through so many changes since its inception. The land, bought in 1859 by Colonel Charles Stuart, was named Glen to describe the peaceful, narrow valley, and Ellen, after his wife. The railroad came in 1879 bringing weekend tourists from San Francisco to rest in the comfortable valley filled with grapevines and medicinal hot springs. Tourists drank the wine and the mineral water, soaking themselves in the comforts of nature.

Many changes I have witnessed from the comfort of my car, and it was a good thing that I learned to accept change because in my area it's hard to keep up with all the new acres and acres of pastoral

151

grape land: new varietal plantings, new pruning techniques, and new vineyard crews. The evolution of this one small plant is quite remarkable. What once started in Europe as a Eurasian species called Vitis vinifera, producing varieties that we are familiar with like Chardonnay, Riesling, Sauvignon Blanc, Gewürztraminer, Pinot Noir, Cabernet Sauvignon, Merlot, and Cabernet Franc, was brought to America by early settlers and accidentally crossed with American varieties, thus producing French-American hybrids. Some of those French-American hybrids include Cayuga, Seyval Blanc, Aurora, and Chancellor, which are more disease-resistant and heartier for certain regions within the United States. It's all about adaptability and change.

Even though change has occurred, farmers must be prudent about what they plant, the trellis system they use, and the techniques they choose, because in Sonoma County commercial grape-growers can't always afford to experiment with all these different varieties; instead, they must follow the demand and produce what is trendy and popular. That means Chardonnay, Pinot Noir, Sauvignon Blanc, Merlot, Syrah, Cabernet Sauvignon, and Zinfandel. And as a general rule, Cabernet Sauvignon and Zinfandel require a longer ripening period and do better in warmer regions, and Chardonnay, Pinot Noir, Sauvignon Blanc, Merlot, and Syrah have a shorter ripening period and can be grown in cooler regions. But growers are beginning to take risks with what variety they plant based on their climate—even if the regional temperatures don't necessarily coincide with their variety.

Training systems have changed, too. The move to produce more fruit and increase the productivity of the grapevines was once the goal for farmers. Grape-growers wanted to manage their land economically, with the almighty dollar at the center of the picture. Gone was the grace and low production of the old head-trained style.

But things have changed once again. Quantity is not necessarily the main goal of grape-growers: there are many new vineyards being planted, competition is tough, and consumer tastes have changed. Consumers want high-quality, interesting wines—and to achieve that winemakers must start with high-quality grapes. Grapevines that are trained and pruned to produce high tonnages (generally over five tons per acre) historically do not produce complex, full-bodied fruit.

Even my own vineyard has taken a different turn. After absorbing the literature of the mid-1980s, I decided to plant our new vines on spiffy trellis systems I learned from the guru of canopy management, Dr. Richard Smart. His ideas were innovative and sound for many growers, but for those like me, who would probably be better off starting a French-style pottery business, most of his systems required certain attributes: fertile soils and vigorous vines. Admittedly, I had neither. We are in a highly stressed region, and training these vines on trellis systems that ask for nine to twelve feet of growth per season is virtually impossible. I found this out the hard way, which resulted in my having to rip out my new trellis systems.

The Geneva Double Curtain (GDC), developed by Professor Nelson Shaulis and so named because it was developed at the Cornell University's Geneva Experiment Station, was one system I chose for my newly planted vines. The GDC is best used for medium to high vigor vines and is a horizontally trained system that has shoots trained to grow downward (an unnatural process since shoots gen-

HOW TO DETERMINE THE VARIETIES BEST SUITED TO THE REGION WHERE YOU LIVE

1. Check U.S. Agricultural Yearbooks: The yearbooks accumulate data on soil and crops on a yearly basis.

2. New York Agricultural Testing Station at Geneva or U.C. Davis: These are experiment stations with information on viticulture.

3. Call around to local nurseries and ask what varieties are being grown in your area.

4. If you live in a commercial grape-growing region, talk to some of the growers about their successes and failures with certain varieties.

erally want to grow toward the sun); nonetheless, it works well for many growers who have the necessary vigor to grow vines that extend nine to twelve feet. Again, *what was I thinking?*

The second system I merrily installed, and unwillingly ripped out, was called the Ruakura Twin Two Tier system, a.k.a. RT2T, reminiscent of the android Star Wars character. But this option was also bad for my area; the system was developed for highly fertile vineyards in New Zealand by Dr. Richard Smart and is probably an excellent system if one has the right terrain. Hmmm . . . *what was I thinking?*

It all sounded so good: a trellis system that would help me produce large tonnages and high-quality fruit. What more could a grape-grower want? I wanted to believe that these systems would work for me. I wanted to prove that I could boost my soil, and that by some miracle I could overcome the fact that I'm in a highly stressed, hillside region. I was wrong. The barriers were too big for me to hurdle, and I finally realized that my life would be smoother if I picked a trellis system to support the characteristics of my terrain.

Change once again. Needless to say, my new vines had to be recently hacked off—retrofitting, we call it—when I finally understood that they simply were not going to make the necessary growth for these two systems. I was tired of sacrificing vine energy for wood growth and never getting a decent crop. All the vines' labor went into producing height, leaving nothing for fruit production.

My own system has now evolved into a head-trained system with cane pruning and spur pruning. I believe this system is uncomplicated and can work well for all types of soil and terrain situations—not just stressed areas. I guess this is another reason why I have a fondness for the head-trained system; not only does it remind me of the past—the good 'ole days when my biggest worries centered around which French field to lie in and how I could stuff one more precious bottle of Chateauneuf-du-Pape in my tattered backpack—but it's a system I can use in my own vineyard that is simple and adaptable to many different types of soil.

Spring

Wine is bottled poetry.
—*Robert Louis Stevenson*

SPRING IN PARIS

2012

"Pick a number between one and thirty," Monsieur Ramage says, looking directly at me. After nine months of being in class at Le Cordon Bleu, I know that it is hopeless to even think about picking a number because this is Monsieur Ramage's "humorous" (though I don't find it so) way of picking me for the next challenge. I stand up, smooth down any loose hairs, and quickly button my suit coat, hoping my audience can't see my pounding heart. The other students sigh with relief that the job is mine.

It is spring now, a time for newness and hope. Can I succeed after all these month of training and impress the man from Margaux who is here today with a set of world-renowned Bordeaux wines? I've been chosen to do the wine tasting analysis, an internationally accepted protocol which chronicles in detail the *visuel*, or visual; *olfactif* or aromatic; and *gustatif*, or taste of a particular wine—and I must do it in seven minutes or less.

After nearly a year of smelling, swirling, and tasting wine, I should be ready for this task. My mind races back to the first days of class when we learned the six key acids present in wine and the silly French saying to help us remember them. *Tu Marche Comme Les Anciens Soldats* (You Walk Like The Old Soldiers). The *t* in this mnemonic is for tartaric acid, the *m* for malic acid, the *c* for citric acid, the *l* for lactic acid, the *a* for acetic acid, and the *s* for succinic acid. For those who preferred English, we changed the saying to Too Much Chocolate Lets Ass Swell, a phrase not quite as conventional but that nonetheless got the job done. The truth is, right now, I really need to march like an old solder in order to pull off a traditionally perfect wine analysis in front of the conventional Margaux man.

My months of wine training and wine evaluating leave my thoughts again, and I feel like a fish out of water. I am climbing a mountain, and I don't want to fall even though I know I will inevitably stumble. It's out of sheer embarrassment at the thought of failing in front of Monsieur Ramage, and my peers, that makes me march on with an overwhelming desire: I want to deliver a sensory analysis that will liberate me from my doubts, and that will perhaps leave me with a bit of notoriety.

I will have to begin with a visual analysis, for which we also learned a mnemonic device: Very Clever Is This Stupid Blasted Test Clever Clever. These nine words correspond with the nine elements of the analysis: viscosity (Does the wine move more like oil or juice in the glass?); color (Is the wine white, yellow, red or purple?); intensity (What is the depth of the wine's color?); tint (What stage in its lifespan is the wine?); surface (How thick are the legs of the wine running down the glass?); brightness (Is the wine bright and clear or dark and cloudy?); transparency (Is the wine-making quality apparent in the overall structure, color, and health of the wine?);

capillary action (How fast do the legs of the wine run?); and carbon dioxide release (Is there gas in the wine?).

The second element of the tasting analysis is the olfactory analysis, for which I will have to take a couple of quick sniffs before I swirl the wine and a couple of sniffs after I swirl the wine. I'll ask myself, is the wine intense and burning, flabby and frail, or abundant with finesse? I will provide my audience with a description of the wine's smell before and after it is swirled, and then I will make a conclusion about the smells.

Next I'll begin my favorite part, the *gustatif*, or tasting step, and I will finally get to sip the wine after staring at it, swirling it, and smelling it. I'll begin by eloquently describing the three phases that occur once the wine enters my mouth: attack, my first impression at the first few moments of entry; development, the changes the wine undergoes after the first few moments in my mouth; and finish, the conclusion of flavors after tasting the wine. After I deliver these observations, I will describe the structure, balance, length, and harmony of the wine, and then I'll finally make a conclusion about the wine—something like, "This wine reminds me of Christmas dinner in the dead of winter because of its boldness and earthiness."

Let me note that I never really got the hang of "chewing" my wine or sucking air through my lips at this stage, as so many wine connoisseurs like to do. Whenever I attempted either of these tasting techniques, I usually stumbled on my mountainside by accidently dribbling wine down my chin or choking when I inhaled the fruity liquid, so I will not do either of these things during my analysis today. Nonetheless, these methods can be useful for anyone who prefers to use them.

And then, to complete my wine analysis, I must not forget to talk about the future of the wine in terms of predicting how it will age, what its serving temperature should be, whether to carafe it, decant it, or leave it alone, and finally, what dish would be best to pair it with.

"Madame Moulton, please proceed," I hear Monsieur Ramage say. I hold the glass of Chateau Kirwan Bordeaux in my hand like a singer ready to begin a melody.

"Good afternoon, *Mesdames et Monsieurs*," I say, standing at the front of the small room, "I am happy to be here today to tell you about this joyous glass of wine." I speak clearly and precisely, making certain to look the members of my audience in the eyes and shift my gaze rhythmically around the room. I want to make everyone feel as though they are sharing this glass of wine with me.

"The color of this wine is a lovely ruby red; it is a solid, deep color, quite shiny and dense," I say. I gracefully give the glass one twist, holding the stem lightly between my thumb and index finger. I smile at my audience and continue. "The legs are thick and clear and run slowly down the sides of the glass, indicating a high level of glycerol and concentrated levels of alcohol. The disk is pronounced in thickness, but there is no color change from the middle of the glass to the edge. In conclusion, the wine is young, clear, and bright, and it is from a terroir filled with high levels of sunshine and daily brightness, encouraging its deep, vibrant red color," I say. I know that I have not hit all ten of the visuals, but I'm close enough to gain a passing mark.

Taste, taste, taste . . . but don't taste wine before you smell it. This dialog is politely repeating itself over and over in my head as I begin the second step of a perfect wine tasting in front of the smiling representative of the Margaux region.

I clear my throat and smile, feeling as though I have climbed a few rocks on this mountain and have not stumbled yet. I take a sniff, and I say, "The first nose reveals smoke, and peppery notes with not many aromas of fruit." I elegantly swirl three times and slowly raise the glass to my nose, sniffing quickly once and then again. "Upon aeration," I say, "the wine opens to reveal intricate smells of black currant, mushrooms, black pepper, and exotic spices." I conclude that the wine has smells that are bold and powerful, reminding me of a meadow in the fall strewn with tall trees and fallen damp leaves; it's bucolic but sophisticated at the same time. I tell my audience this wine would be lovely served on a wintry day, and I imagine out loud that I would enjoy it while sitting by my stone fireplace, my dog at my feet, with the smells of fresh bread wafting in from the kitchen.

The room is quiet, my audience waiting for my next comments and wondering whether I can continue on with my love story about this wine. I am ready to taste, and I take my first sip. "The attack is voluminous and at the same time smooth," I expound, "and it develops nicely with a symphony of fruit, ending in a long hearty finish lasting five to seven seconds." I quickly continue, "The tannins are not overly obtrusive and are structurally balanced well with the fruit flavors, acid, and alcohol." I finish by saying that this wine unveils flavors of aged black currant, spice, and black pepper, and that it opens up into a structurally magnificent balance of racy, yet complex finesse.

I am nearly done with the analysis, and I'm sweating profusely under my black suit. I am not sure if I can dramatize this wine for one more second. I feel that my choice of words may have been too adventurous and in the end may get me into trouble.

Monsieur Ramage nods his head and signals me to go on. I carry on about the temperature at which to serve the wine, and I say that the wine could be decanted for a few minutes in order to open up its complex flavors.

"This youthful and forward 2009 Bordeaux from Chateau Kirwan, which is predominantly Cabernet Sauvignon blended with Merlot, Petite Verdot, and Cabernet Franc," I exclaim, "could be paired with a lovely garlic-rubbed grilled leg of lamb served with roasted rosemary potatoes and sautéed green beans with toasted pine nuts . . ."

Monsieur Ramage is proudly smiling at me and begins to clap.

"Or," I sheepishly announce over the first seconds of applause, "it could be paired with a thin-crusted pizza covered with caramelized onions, crispy pancetta, sautéed shitake mushrooms, and Gorgonzola cheese."

I become infamous in France, or at least at Le Cordon Bleu, on that day for my adventurous food and wine pairing. My classmates snicker, but they are secretly happy that I've broken tradition, and they congratulate me for days after the episode.

"Why you do that!" Monsieur Ramage shouts at me after my offbeat pairing suggestion. "You just gave perfect wine analysis and then ruined it by your food pairing . . . *pizza, mon Dieu*, not with Chateau Kirwan from Margaux!"

"Why not?" I mutter quietly so he can't hear me.

I feel vindicated after all these months of following traditional food and wine pairings because I have gained enough respect to confidently step out of my safe haven and add some adventure. Since I feel that I have done well on my analysis of this Chateau Kirwan Bordeaux—a very expensive and elite red wine—ending it with a traditional suggested pairing of lamb, I think that my suggestion to pair it with pizza is acceptable. More importantly, I believe that a bottle of Chateau Kirwan would actually pair well with a gourmet pizza. I make a note to myself to try this combination once I return to the States!

I have set myself apart in the world of food and wine not by breaking the rules from the beginning but by learning all the traditions of food and wine pairing and then branching out once I felt certain of my technical knowledge. After many months of struggle, I have become not just a technical dancer of food and wine but also a modern dancer of food and wine. I am finally liberated.

NINE

WHEN LIFE GIVES YOU SOUR GRAPES, MAKE SWEET WINE

2003

*S*pring, glorious spring, a momentous occasion in the wine country. The static hush of winter is gone and the fruitful smells of spring unexpectedly appear—the first impalpable signal that winter is over. The fertile scents come from sprouting grasses, blooming daffodils, and germinating mustard fields, and they are carried by the wind across the countryside. Hidden within those riveting fragrances there resides a mellifluous symphony of sounds bursting forth with the spirit and bang of a well-crafted concert. These electrifying whiffs and arousing noises are the conveyors that suggest the arrival of a new season. Like Paul Revere riding into town carrying news, their trailing perfumes and joyful music disseminate energizing information.

These are the intangible signs that imply it's time for the grape-vines to awaken, that soon the intensity of color and rapid growth of the vine will beckon the observer like a friendly invite to a wayfaring newcomer. "Get-up-and-go," the eye-catching vine says, "come meet me and soak up the pleasure of watching me grow." The grapevines' essence is contagious and flows down to every form of life.

I've spent many days in awe of all the smells and sounds of springtime. But I must admit, there are some tradeoffs associated with my wonder-struck country impressions; exchanges that have particularly impacted my life when it comes to sleep. During this time of year I do spend many a wakeful night wondering if I'll ever get any rest. I never had such worries when I lived in the city. But there are just too many critters hanging around with too many fervent spring sounds bellowing from their throats—both day and night. The frogs and wild turkeys seem to be the biggest offenders, and they are the loudest around midnight, their croaking reverberations and cackling jangles echoing throughout my house. I've often tried opening my bedroom window to yell at them to make them hush, but this only stops their crusades for a few moments. As soon as I shut the window and climb back into bed they begin again, starting slowly with a controlled melody that finally lapses bringing on the same deafening loudness. I lay in bed waiting for the next stanza to come and it always does. I've grown accustom to this spring commotion, and just as a city person learns to sleep through traffic noises, I've learned to ignore the recitals and get down to the business of sleep.

I haven't, however, grown accustom to the havoc that deviating spring weather can cause when it comes to my grapevines. And although my earlier pithy description of these months outlines the way it usually occurs in the Sonoma wine country, there have been many exceptions. Which is why I still confront springtime weather with trepidation, and I sweat my way through the erratic behavior of this most venerable season. In the beginning, I didn't approach spring with any fear whatsoever, but I'm shamed to say that as my years in farming progress, I've developed an uncanny dread for the coming of this season. It all started about four years ago, when, after having lived through six springs that had succinctly followed the unremarkable guidelines of conducive farming weather, I was awakened to the underlying catastrophes that a variant spring can cause to grapes as well as one's comfortable life. That particular year, spring did indeed approach as expected: the winds blew arousing bouquets; the frogs and turkeys began squawking; the blush of floral colors impregnated the ground; but then the skies opened up and dumped snow. The plants got confused and thought it was still winter, the animals belched and burped and hid in the bushes, and the air smelled like a freezing ice rink—void of the sweet, fertile vigor of bloom.

I knew that the snow was bad for the bud-breaking grapevines, since it would cause the fragile buds to freeze and disallow any decent future production of fruit for that year, but it was nothing compared to the emotional storm that came immediately after the snow flurry. Dawn was just breaking and my family was awakened to a rumpus that sounded as though a plane had crashed in our living room. We all jumped from our beds and clung to the comfort of one another. We found, much to our surprise, that our dwelling was intact but that a bolt of lightning had struck a very large tree and charred it midway down, causing it to splinter and crash onto a bridge that runs across a small creek through our yard. The howl

169

that split our ears and startled us out of our blissful sleep was the roaring sound of thunder that came soon after, followed by the high-pitched squeal the tree made as it snapped off into pieces and smashed into the side of the wooden bridge.

Grace, Dude, and Joy were horrified that the powerful spring storm had caused a huge tree to fall so dangerously close to our home, missing us by only a small distance, and I was forlorn about my crop that would surely be damaged by the frozen grapevine buds. There was no power or water for days, and to top it off Rachel was coming back for a visit from England. She'd been gone over a year and we were anxiously awaiting her arrival.

"This was not supposed to happen," I tearfully told Chuck. "It's spring and we just shouldn't have to deal with cantankerous elements." We had been lucky thus far; I had become immune to the effects of capricious seasons and because of this I was complacent about the effects of weather on country living and grape-growing. I knew nothing other than smooth spring transitions we had experienced for the last six years.

"Don't worry, she'll understand," he said trying to soothe me. "I know you can make the most out of this sour situation." This was so ironic since her many years spent with us entailed days where we both became scouts looking for the missing pieces of country living—searching for water, for the animals that had committed crimes against our domain, and for what we thought would be the simplest way for novice country homesteaders to survive.

I knew that Rachel was looking forward to this jaunt to California—we all were—and I was genuinely disappointed. Long before she left, we had carefully worked it out so that she could rotate her seasons with us. One year she would spend a month in the fall, the next year a month in the winter, and so on. This would make us all feel like she'd never miss a season, but it also meant that when she came we all expected the season to behave appropriately.

"We have a slight predicament, Rach," I calmly told her as I opened the car door for her at San Francisco International curbside. I thought I better tell her right away that she wouldn't have a hot shower or a warm bed or toasty spring weather.

She quickly scanned my body looking for signs of injury. "What have you done now, you wild girl?"

"Nothing," I said. "I'm fine, really." She was still apprehensive. I couldn't blame her since her first three months in California had been spent as my nursemaid. While I lounged around on the couch gritting my teeth and whining about the pain, she ran herself ragged running errands, cooking, cleaning, and consoling me. Though I'd demand that she drink my voluminous red wines and I told her how much I appreciated her, I felt tremendously guilty about her working so hard.

"Okay, then, did the mountain lion come back?" she asked.

She was referring to an incident that happened one year when she and Joy had been on their way to the mailbox. Rachel spotted a mountain lion standing twenty yards above on the hillside. She didn't want to alarm Joy and she knew that if they ran it would encourage the animal to chase them as their prey. It had been a blustery day that threatened rain and they both had on rain jackets, so she quickly unbuttoned her coat and opened her slicker, holding the jacket open on both sides letting the expansion of the material flap in the wind. She slowly turned in circles. The goal was to scare

TIPS FOR COOLER REGIONS AND COLD SPRING WEATHER

Late pruning—February to March—delays budburst by up to three weeks. In drastically cooler regions don't prune vines until immediately after buds begin swelling. This will maybe avoid the potential of frost death.

At first pruning, leave double the canes and after bud break, hopefully when there is no longer any more threat of frost, go back and prune off dead buds, using the extra canes as back-up for the lost buds (end product will have total number of buds you originally planned on).

For free-standing vines trained low to the ground, the vines can be laid in trenches and covered with straw after fall. Remove or straighten them once the weather warms up.

Choose a grape variety that can withstand cold. *Vitis vinifera* can only handle as cold as 10 degrees Fahrenheit during dormancy, but some American varieties can handle -10 degrees Fahrenheit.

Create a sheltering environment by laying rocks and rocklike debris around the vines. Rocks provide heat once they are warmed from the sun, and in the fall they control the weeds by acting as a barrier.

the animal by making the two of them look bigger. "Look, Joy, let's dance," she said. Joy did the same with her coat and they twisted and turned, gyrating around slowly. The animal stopped moving toward them and slinked its way up the mountain, turning its head to look

In cooler regions, plant the vines from southeast to southwest. This maximizes the benefits of light and sun exposure.

Plant vines closer together in order to increase the density of foliage and block or capture the sunlight for the leaves—before it hits the soil.

Train the vine to grow higher off the ground and this will insure that the plant is further away from the colder air on the ground.

TIPS FOR WARMER REGIONS AND HOT SPRING WEATHER

When temperatures become too hot the problem of high temperatures can be alleviated by irrigating the vines at bloomtime. Irrigation cycles of three minutes on, twelve minutes off, will cool the air but not water the vines. Keep the water off the vines because water could interfere with the flow of energy within the vine and shift it to shoot growth instead of fruit development.

In warmer regions, plant the vines from northeast to northwest. Plant vines further apart so that the sunlight will penetrate the soil and the heat will be more dispersed.

back several times. Joy was so excited about the new dance that she never saw the animal.

"Nope. You'll be safe walking down to the mailbox." I said laughing. "I haven't seen any mountain lions since you left."

Rachel looked around the car at Grace, Dude, and Joy. "Okay, so everyone seems healthy and happy. The hair looks good, the clothes are white, and I don't see any remnants of previous injuries." We had picked her up one time and all of our hair was orange from the high levels of iron in our well water. She had thought this was very funny until her month stay was over and she left with peach hair and tea-rose clothes.

"Do you give up?" I asked.

"Go on, what is it?" she questioned. "I'm out of ideas."

"Well, it's not a big deal, really, but you're just going to have to pretend it's winter instead of spring," I said. "And then next year we'll adjust the schedule accordingly and you can come back again in the spring." I thought this was brilliant and a great way to outsmart the corrupt seasons.

"I'm so relieved. That's nothing," she said.

We cooked prawns with calabrian chilis and sweet peppers covered with fresh cilantro and a rich tarragon cream sauce, steamed artichokes with lemon aioli and anchovy paste, and asparagus with sweet balsamic vinegar and soy sauce; we drank from my special stash of wines. Since the weather was still behaving like winter, I pulled out a bottle of Coturri Zinfandel, a blend of ninety percent dry-farmed, organic Zin with ten percent Sangiovese. It's a wine made from fruit grown in my mountains—the Sonoma Mountains—by Phil Coturri, one of the leading organic viticulturists in Sonoma County, filled with enough personality to cover an entire page with explicative expressions beyond most connoisseurs wildest imaginations. Dry-farmed grapes have profoundly layered individuality. Some farmers say this is because the grapevine roots must go deep in search of water, and on their way to find water they pick up complex features that are passed on to the flavors of the grapes. But a farmer willing to take the dry-farming risk is visionary, insightful, and unconcerned with money; instead, they care mostly about flavor, and grasping the complexity of Mother Nature without the turmoil of monetary concerns.

I told Rachel the story about the lightning, and apologized profusely about the fact that we'd be without power or water for three or four days. "At least we can still cook," I said. She was unconcerned. "But the frogs are here for you, Rachel," I added as consolation. We enthusiastically wait for their arrival each year; it means that winter has officially turned to spring. And that year, despite the confusion and mixed messages from Mother Nature, they were here, which was a great relief.

"Thank God," she laughed, "I was worried I'd have to wait another whole year to hear them."

Every spring—sunshine or snow—the croakers begin serenading, and I've found that their concerts usually consist of a menagerie of spitting frogs, mating frogs, and a loud band of all different types of frogs hoarsely quacking unique tunes. For some strange reason this always seems to happen at the same time the delicious aromas of spring arrive and my grapevines' buds are ready to explode. I've studied this correlation between frog and grapevine by monitoring the exact date the buds burst and the frogs start croaking. Collecting this data inevitably forced me to come face-to-face with some pretty gnarly looking bullfrogs. Bulging eyes and olive-green spotted bodies, these amphibians exhibit not one ounce of aggression or misdoubt from my presence. But I do admit that it's a bit unnerving when they stick out their tongues and spit—what must be foul-tasting insects—at me. Nonetheless, the research I've done on frogs says that mating season, the time when those critters become vocal, begins with spring rains. But this is simply not true for the frogs on my farm. Their mating season begins when grapevine budburst occurs.

It happens this way every year and I like this non-technical signal, most of the time, except when I'm trying to have a peaceful (quiet) dinner party. One year I grilled up platters of salmon and marinated vegetables with chipotle and mango salsa, and served my guests glasses of Syrah made by Steele Wines from the fruit managed by Steve Hill, a meticulous grower, well known in the valley. I hoped the wine would induce conversation enough to drown out the vibrating background noises. This technique had worked on occasion for short periods. I discovered that it made no difference whether we dined outside or inside because the frogs had learned to heighten their barks to such a level that not even a closed door muffles them. My friends marveled at how vociferous the noisy frogs could be, and they laughed about the exotic background music they provided while we ate. As guests departed, I begged them to grab one, stuff it in a jar, and tote it off to their city dwelling. "You don't like the sound of the frogs?" they joked. "I do," I sighed, which was true, "but I just wish they'd stop when we have friends over."

So on my farm, when the frogs start making sounds, we wait for the vines to come alive. I consider myself lucky to have this special notification system alerting me to the approaching bud growth (not all grape-growers have this). But if I didn't have my frogs, budburst would happen when the mean daily temperature becomes 50 degrees Fahrenheit—usually in late March or early April—depending upon the weather in a given year. Grapevine budburst is a springtime ritual that invites the grower to view the wonderwork of Mother Nature. Sometimes the shoots will burst forth with such vigor that they may even grow one inch in a day.

Despite my trepidation about early spring, I look forward to budburst because it means another year of growth for my vines. Age means good things for grapevines: more fruit, more beauty, and more character. The first two to three weeks after bud break there may be anywhere from six to eight leaves with one new flower cluster. By eight weeks the shoot is well on its way, and the leaves and flower clusters are formed. The flow of carbohydrates in a young growing shoot changes as the shoot lengthens. At the beginning of shoot growth the energy comes from carbohydrates that have been stored through the winter, but once the leaves appear the shoots' energy comes from the leaves.

And when the frogs stop croaking—around mid-May to early June—frog mating season is over, budburst is complete, and bloom begins. Bloom occurs when the average temperature is around 65 degrees Fahrenheit and the light exposure increases. But for me, the process of bloom—when it's time for the grapevines' shoot growth to slow down and flowers to bloom on the shoots (flowers are in clusters that will later form the grape bunches)—takes place when the frogs stop their nightly musicals.

After budburst and bloom, the frogs remain in my yard but their notification services are terminated. So I'm on my own when it comes to determining exactly when berry development will occur. But it's generally around eight weeks from the start of bloom—

around mid-July—when berry development or *veraison* begins. *Veraison* is a French word that describes the color change that takes place during berry development. This entire process, from berry set to the day the fruit is picked, can last anywhere from ten to nineteen weeks. Some years my crop has been ready for harvest by late August, and other years the ripe fruit is frighteningly close to Thanksgiving and the threat of damaging winter rain.

Having lived through ten years of grape-growing in spring, I've learned to recognize not only the benefits of blooming grapevines, but the virtues of frog wildlife and their sophisticated notification structure. I once read that frogs are considered to be symbols of good luck in Japan. The frogs in my vineyard, despite the disquietude they furnish, have brought me good fortune with their charming information system. They notify me of imminent budburst, and they let me know when bloom will occur. And because of them, I've come to understand that I don't own the views of nature; I certainly don't own the frogs; I don't own the brilliance of springtime; I just own the rhapsody that ensues. And for that I am most grateful.

BLOOMTIME

At bloom, the flower has the role of transforming the flower clusters into grape clusters. These special flowers have four integral parts. The first is the calyx, generally composed of five sepals, or the protective tissue of the flower. They quickly disappear and are present only to protect the flower parts as the process of bloom begins. The second is the corolla, also known as the calyptra, flower petals, or cap of the flower. The flower petals can have anywhere from five to nine petals. The third is the stamens, and the fourth is the pistil. The stamens are the male or pollen center for the flower, and the pistil is the female part containing the stigma, style, and ovary of the plant. (All of these terms are shared by many different types of flowers.)

During bloom, which usually lasts anywhere from seven to ten days but deviations do occur, the cap or petals of the flower peel away from the bottom of the flower and fly off. If rain occurs during this brief period, the cap cannot fly off and the flowers may be unable to set in order to continue the process of berry development. However, rain at this time doesn't always cause this disaster because all of the clusters may not bloom at the same time. Some clusters may bloom a week before others. This is a safeguard against total crop loss, since the chances of rain at all times during bloom are probably slim.

Once the flowers open and the caps fly off, the pollination process begins. The stamens and the pistil begin their work. A portion of the pistil—the stigma—becomes sticky and the pollen is released from the stamen. The pollen needs to reach the stigma. The stickiness of the stigma allows the pollen to stick. If rain occurs at this time, the pollen cannot stick to the stigma and the crop will suffer for that year, or it can cause dilution of the stigma leaving the egg unfertilized. Since grapevines are self-pollinating; everything needed to produce a crop is contained within each plant.

The final process of bloom is fertilization. This process allows the set of the berries. After pollination, a pollen tube is produced that grows into the egg cell, or ovary. Three nuclei come down and end up in the egg. One of these becomes the embryo of the seed, and the other two become the food source for the seed. The cell division allows seed development and berry enlargement. For the pollen tube to grow, there must be temperatures anywhere from 65–85 degrees Fahrenheit, supplied energy, and boron.

TEN

A WELL HALF EMPTY

*T*here's a ghost running around my property messing with the buttons on my water controls," I jokingly told my well man, Gil, one spring, my pink cell phone smashed to my ear as I trudged through clumps of mud and plant debris (probably poison oak). Snooping around my 10,000-gallon water tank—that never has any water—is my favorite solo pastime for Friday afternoons. He has come to expect my weekly phone call. "I'm stumped, again, but the tank is empty just in time for Saturday," I tell him. "Right on schedule for another weekend without water."

"What happened this time?" Gil asks, laughing into the receiver. I laugh, too, as I dribble my way through a long, distorted discussion about why I think we have no water. I usually tease him with ridiculous commentaries about supernatural forces pressing water control buttons and invading my serenity. He is good-natured and always humors me.

"Yes, but did someone turn a valve, did a pipe break, did an animal plug the well shaft?" he inquires. These are the logical reasons why my water could be missing; they are much too rational for me to comprehend.

Water was a mystery to me when I first moved to the country. I never really thought about where it was coming from, how long it would last, and what it was composed of—until I didn't have any. Prior to moving to Glen Ellen, water had always been there when I turned on the faucet; it was there when I pushed my garden irrigation switches. It was only after the water was gone from my farm that I realized how much I desperately needed it.

The reasons for our missing water—whether natural or supernatural—were endless. And I'm not proud of all the nagging phone calls I made to the well company almost every Friday afternoon. The well company's job was to dig wells, not find my missing water. But with the kids gone to school, Chuck at work, and Rachel back to England, there was just Bubba and I at home to take care of business. I never asked them to dig me a new well; instead, I asked them to help me find where my water had gone. I started inquiring about how to make more water from my existing source.

"Couldn't we figure out a way to salvage what we already have?" I kept asking Gil, hoping he would have more insight than I had. "There must be more water where that came from." He remained supportive; nevertheless, it became like asking a dentist to cure a repressed fear just because he works on something close to your brain. Since I spent so much of my time in search of missing water, hungering for a shower like a gold digger yearning for gold, it impacted my ability to see the truth. I continued to ask for help, and

Gil continued to give it. I learned to swallow my pride, because without his help I'd be driving around all weekend shuttling family members back and forth to public showers, restaurants, and the homes of our closest friends. I couldn't even fathom this thought.

The water was not always lost when I made those bothersome phone calls to the well company, and sometimes (if I was lucky) I did actually know the whereabouts of my water long before I contacted them for help. Take the day when I was headed to the shower and I noticed a deliveryman driving down our road. Craning to see if he bore some spectacular gift for me, I temporarily postponed my shower. Upon realizing it was only some running shoes I had ordered for myself, I headed for the shower again. As I reached for my towel, there was a loud noise that caught my attention. I streaked to a nearby window and found him standing outside his truck—that had veered off our road into a ditch—shoving his hand over a giant swelling of water that was spewing onto the road.

"No!" I screamed, scrunching down on the floor because I still had no clothes on.

He ran off the road by accident, he apologized, and swiped the handle on one of the water valves, the result being 10,000 gallons of stored water flowing down our hillside. This might have been good had it been time to irrigate the grapevines, but it was spring and the skies were still dumping huge amounts of water.

Then there was the time when I was driving home down my private country road dreamily staring out my car window, hoping to catch a glimpse of the spectacular morning sunshine dancing across the fields. Instead I spotted water spouting twenty feet in the air. One of the irrigation pipes had sprung a leak, not a trickle, but a seepage of such great magnitude that after a few hours our water supply was completely gone. This would not have been odd if we had been using our irrigation system, but we had disconnected it two years before because we didn't have enough water. Who hit that switch?

I'm proud to say that I discovered these types of situations on my own without the expert detective work needed from my well people. These were the rewarding times when I was pleased to make the diagnosis, when I didn't have to flash my vulnerability and fan my ignorance like a helpless person in distress.

Over the years, though, there have been many other hapless situations when switches, valves, and buttons were pushed and turned the wrong way, but I wasn't the great discoverer who made the final determination. No, indeed, I had to call in well experts to help me locate the hidden problem, which is probably why I insist on giving newcomers and visitors the same speech, "You can touch the grapevines, you can touch the oak trees, you can touch the animals (if you can catch them), but don't touch or push any buttons, hidden valves, or handles anywhere on this property." Some people laugh at me and others just smile politely and nod in agreement.

✳ ✳ ✳

People who don't live nearby or know my family wouldn't know that water mishaps were once so commonplace on our property that we were forced to survive for an entire year off the water from one single garden hose. There were so many broken pipes running from the well to the storage tank, and twisted valves leaking water all over the mountainside, and irrigation switches on unauthorized schedules, that we couldn't ever seem to get our holding tank full enough to supply water for the house. So we remedied this by taking water directly from the well—via a single garden hose—circumventing all the old problems.

Taking water directly from the well was not a great way to live because there was no filtering, no refining, and no guarantee that debris—sticks, dirt, or even small snakes—might not make their way through the faucet to our house. Even so, we worried more about an animal plugging our small garden hose opening, stopping the flow of precious water into our house, than seeing a snake in the toilet.

But there's really not enough water from a garden hose for a family of five, and to make it work we had to scrutinize every drop of water that was used, carefully conserving (for a year) everything that came through that tiny rubber pipe. Our life was much like camping without the beauty of actually being outdoors. We rarely got showers, we had to relieve ourselves outside, and we mostly ate hiker-style from a can.

Nonetheless, we survived because these were seemingly uncomplicated problems that could be fixed by patching pipes, firing certain delivery people, and removing water-seeking animals. Unfortunately, there have been other water issues—complicated, frustrating problems—that no one, not even the well people, could figure out. Did the water venture off to the neighbors for a more peaceful existence? Or meander to adjacent farmlands to watch grazing cows and slumbering cats? Or get sucked into the ground with all the other elements of the earth? None of us knew.

Despite the unfair disruption it caused, I learned to live with the absurdity of our water situation and to ponder this ridiculous conundrum bestowed upon my family and farm. While I searched across acres of land looking for hiding water (there are many places to look with seven acres of vineyard irrigation, an acre of backyard drip lines, and hundreds of feet of pipes that run underground up a vast hillside that leads from the well to a holding tank), I realized that there must be some hidden meaning as to why I've been forced to spend so many wasted hours in hot pursuit of runaway water.

We are all stubborn in this household, and rather than drill for a new well—a costly approach that requires lots of risk—we opted to find another way, a direction taken only by the fearless and adventurous who believe in the goodness of sacrifice. We were ready to experience new ways to deal with our water shortage, which involved sacrificing our comfort to learn new truths, putting our selfish needs aside in order to understand more about our inner selves, and discovering our biggest weaknesses and greatest fears. All this in an effort to become stronger, better people who were concerned about protecting our environment by not making unnecessary demands on its resources.

And so the many hours I spent looking for lost water weren't really wasted afterall. While I traipsed through the underbrush of my land, I listed my alternatives under my breath, refusing to accept the fact that my well was dwindling down to nothing. Instead, I devised a brilliant plan for surviving with our declining water: rigid household shower schedules, laundry done at the local Laundromat, toilets flushed only when absolutely necessary, and all irrigation (vineyard included) shut off. We were ready for the battle; we would beat the odds; we would outlast the impertinence of that well. Mother Nature would not destroy us. Our heartiness would prevail.

Heartiness, we learned, is not an inborn trait, but rather a characteristic that one discovers—hopefully—after struggling through a serious crisis. The bottom line: Some people find this quality and others never do. Which is probably why only some members of my family understood that long, twice-a-day showers were no longer a right. This unavoidably led to lots of door-banging and nasty accusations about who used up all the water. I kept reminding my children that we were doing this for the betterment of ourselves (I'm not sure they ever believed that) and the advancement of our land.

Consequently, all of us experienced a major life change. We no longer took the things that nature had to offer for granted. The natural resources on our property were ours to use, but they were not ours to waste. This meant that our household useages were curbed, and it meant I had to reckon with the demands I had placed on my family, and carry them through to the vineyard. My strict, yearly irrigation schedules had to be abandoned.

I was forced to dry farm my vineyard. Dry farming is a term farmers use that means exactly what it says: no water for the farm. It's a complicated alternative that can cause pain and sacrifice for even the heartiest of farmers. But because of my newfound principles on water (we could conserve without digging a new well) and because I believed that somehow Mother Nature would protect me (dump water when my grapevines needed it, and provide long, warm summers with cool, foggy, rejuvenating evenings), I took the risk. I also kept the hope in the back of my mind that if the grapes managed to thrive they would produce extravagant berries with flavors rivaled by no irrigated grape.

Chuck accepted my reasons for not digging a new well and I went on believing that our lack of water was a nonentity in our lives—a minor nuisance and an insignificant technical problem that would resolve itself if we kept a positive attitude and continued to believe in the goodness of nature. I was hopeful, and I insisted that the rest of the family remain optimistic. So what if I lost my humility when it came to asking the well people for help? My mind was clouded with good cheer and a sanguine outlook. I was in a blissful state of denial; it's a pleasant place to be that affords one the luxury of being happy—with or without water.

After all, many winemakers say that when grapevines are given little or no water they produce extraordinary, flavorful wines. And besides, I told myself, a new well would cost many thousands of dollars, and I preferred to invest my money in finding better ways to farm, and hopefully a more insightful pathway that used techniques that were innovative and unknown. I was reminded of when Jack London was raising pigs on the mountain next to me and he tried to create, through lots of time and endless research, a cactus with no needles or prickly leaves. The cactus would grow without much water and at the same time it would be an economical way to feed his pigs. It was a great concept—even if he couldn't get the plant to thrive.

After my second year of dry farming, just as London figured out that growing his spineless cactus was not prudent, I realized that growing grapes without irrigation might not be wise for me, either. This revelation, despite my personal water needs, ethical desire to conserve our well, and wholehearted belief that my grapes would be more complex without water, finally came to me when I attended my annual spring growers' luncheon at Ravenswood Winery, an event that is put on yearly to honor the grapegrowers who sell their fruit to Ravenswood. Normally, this is an event that growers love. The party is thrown by prestigious winemaker Joel Peterson, astute grower relations manager Diane Kenworthy, and expert viticulturist Don Williams, at an opportune time when there is a lull before the next harvest and before the fruit from last year's crop is ready to be bottled. They make the growers feel special and they impart their belief that good wine must start in the vineyard; bad, disease-infested grapes make bad wine no matter what protocol the winemaker follows. If you are like me, though, a grower who in the past two years had experienced difficult harvests, the gay atmosphere can make you feel envious and disheartened.

"So ... Paula Moulton ... can we expect a sizable crop from you this year?" The words came from Don Williams as I picked up my nametag from the sign-in table.

"Well, you see," I started in, "everything was going along really smoothly until around mid-summer when the grape clusters just broke from their shoots and fell to the ground with a big splat, oozing juice all over my soil. And then, whatever didn't fall off the vine, the wild turkeys and deer gobbled up." I must have sounded like a kid overdramatizing some event by using twisted descriptions and unreserved jargon.

"Really ..." he mused, maybe trying to grasp my non-technical description.

"Yup, what really happened was we ran out of water," I back-pedaled to overcompensate for my previous statement. Afterall, this was the truth, sort of.

A friend standing nearby interjected, "Didn't you see any signs—like the leaves wilting?"

"Yes, but we farm on the edge (the wild, risky side, where optimism triumphs over pessimism which, in this case, meant the crop would prevail even without water) and at the end of summer that's nothing out of the ordinary for me."

"You would have been okay dry farming if the vines had been older and more established," the vineyard expert offered, his technical analysis prompt and assured.

"I know, I know," I said. It was more than excruciating to hear.

"Have you followed good irrigation practices and kept the vines healthy this year?" he questioned, genuinely concerned. "How's it going now, with the water situation and all?"

"Just great," I exclaimed (lying because we were back in the same predicament and, in fact, I'd just spent the last two months fretting about whether to give in and dig a new well or whether to redevelop my old one and salvage what I already had). But it's like being in a receiving line at a wedding where you don't have the time or desire to go into painful details. All my absurd stories about chasing lost water and living off the water from a garden hose seemed irrelevant. Besides, I had to let the other grape-growers, patiently waiting their turn to talk to him, have their time, too.

Moving on to a group of growers talking freely about their last year's crop, we talk about whose grapes are in which bottles of Ravenswood wine and then we taste each other's vintages and gasp at the wonderful flavors of our peers. Because the wine is made separately and then blended, each grower gets a couple of bottles that are made solely from their fruit. (It's also a way to critique the fruit from each vineyard.) I didn't have any wine that year because there was so little of my fruit it wasn't worth bottling it separately; it had to be blended right away. At these lunches we inevitably end up bemoaning the eccentric year we've just experienced, focusing our discussion on our difficult boss—Mother Nature—who can be vicious, erratic, and unforgiving.

Every year there is always someone, during the course of conversation, who gloats about their high tonnages and the quality that came with it. We all know this is wrong. The equation: grapes + high tonnages = high quality simply does not figure. Who are they kidding? I will never fall for that one. But every year, even though I know that I shouldn't, I always ask those growers closest to my farming proximity and soil type: "How many tons do you actually get per acre?" I know this is a dangerous question—akin to asking a parent how bright their child is—and one that some people twist, I'm certain, just to make themselves appear better than the rest. Because if they really knew about what they were saying, they would tell you the tonnages are low, very low, and the quality is high, very high. Yet every year I get a similar answer: "Oh, usually around four to six tons per acre."

"Are you dry farming?" I ask, trying to sound polite as swear words bang around in my head wanting to come out.

"We did this year," they say.

To my friends sitting next to me I whisper what I have just heard, and they shake their heads in disbelief. "That's bullshit," they laughingly say, "there is absolutely no way that dry farming will produce those high tonnages in a highly stressed area.

"Maybe they got their numbers mixed up and meant to say .4 or .6 tons per acre," someone interjects.

After the Ravenswood Winery luncheon, I finally began to understand that if I wanted to play ball with the big boys I'd better figure out a way to produce a crop that didn't drop to the ground before harvest. I'd worry about the finer details of crop size later. This probably meant that I needed at least some water for the vines, and that pooh-poohing this knowledge, acting as if everything would slide into place on its own, was not going to work anymore. I had to accept the fact that water was a crucial element needed for the health and success of comfortable grape-growing (and my family as well). If I were making my own wine, and had many acres of grapes, a half a ton per acre would be okay just as long as the wine was exquisite (ethereal it would no doubt be with all of its life going into a half ton per acre). But I wasn't making my own wine, and I didn't have many acres of grapes, and I had to please Ravenswood by at least making it worth their time to deal with me. During the year, a contracted winery walks the vineyard of their growers, making sure the farmer is doing their job and treating the land right. With a winery like Ravenswood, where there are many thousands of cases being produced, advising and consulting takes up a large portion of their time.

Because of my constraints, I determined that my job as a grape-grower was to provide essential water when the vine needed it and where its roots could absorb it. There was too much risk for me growing grapes without any water simply because my tonnages were too low. I needed to support my grapevines because their soil was composed of rock, clay, and volcanic ash and because they were heavily stressed. Viticulture experts say that grapevines need a minimum (I was dealing with minimums in order to conserve) of twelve inches of water per year. But this is no simple task, because even if an area receives many more than twelve inches of rainfall a year, the soil may have a low availability rate due to infiltration—predominately sandy soil will have low water retention and good drainage, and a predominately clay soil will have high water retention and poor drainage—or the climate may be so warm that the water dissipates immediately after it hits the ground. And wetting the soil to the depth of the grapevines' roots is not so easy either. Where are the roots? Unless you remember how deep you ripped your soil to create space for the roots to grow—before planting the vines—or unless you have x-ray vision that can penetrate through layers of soil and see exactly how deep your roots are, this is a big problem. Deduction could assist: a predominately clay soil may allow the vines' roots to grow down to four feet, a loam soil six to ten feet, and a sandy soil ten feet or more. One inch of water can move through the soil downward and laterally twelve inches in sandy soil, seven inches in loam soil, and five inches in clay soil. With these estimates one can probably produce a working plan (if they know their soil and how deep they ripped their soil before planting). Therefore, grapevines with shallow roots will require shorter irrigations more frequently, and grapevines with deeper roots will need longer irrigations less frequently.

My big question once I found water was, would I be able to tell how much available water was in my root zone and when to irrigate the vines? I could inquire about the rainfall in my area (from county organizations or nurseries), and there are gadgets (I hate gadgets) for this type of thing: resistance blocks, tensiometers, neutron probes, pressure bombs, infra-red guns that measure the amounts of water present in soil where the vines' roots can absorb it. But I discovered that Mother Nature has provided a much easier, more accurate, and cheaper method: visual signs from the vine. This was a major discovery for me, and although it seems simple, it dramatically impacted my farming procedures from that point on. Forget about the textbooks (most of the time) and LOOK at the darn vines. Do they look healthy, do they produce a good crop, do they make me happy?

In essence, there wasn't one juncture that changed my perspective about dry farming my grapes; instead, there were many overshadowing moments strung together. Like a convoluted circus show with clowns, animals, and acrobats all performing simultaneously as the spectators make judgments about their act, my moments—although not so entertaining—allowed me to draw important conclusions from the twisted events. The embarrassment of having very little crop, or watching my unripe grape clusters drop to the ground mid-summer (long before harvest), or witnessing my grapevines' leaves wilt and shrivel at the beginning of their spring growth, were the instants that changed my stubborn ideas and hopeful wishes about farming with no water.

YOUR VINES AND THEIR WATER NEEDS

Reasons Grapevines Need Water

1. Protoplasm of Vine (85–90%)

2. Photosynthesis (vines need light from sun, oxygen from air, and water from soil to produce sugar for energy)

3. Solvent for Nutrients (water dissolves and carries nutrients)

4. Turgidity (keeps internal cell pressure firm)

Five Factors Affecting Infiltration

1. Soil texture: sand, silt, or clay (porous sand has greater infiltration than clay)

2. Organic matter present in soil (encourages infiltration)

3. Moistness of soil (wetter soils have lower infiltration)

4. Temperature of soil (colder soils take in water more slowly)

5. Depth of hard pan, bedrock, or any inhibiting layer

Irrigation procedures are difficult to categorize because there are many variables: temperature of region, type of soil, amount of yearly rainfall. Rather than supply a chart, I'm giving you signs to watch for to help you determine when to irrigate. If your vines are planted in a pot, you need to pay close attention to signs during the year because there is no reserve of water in a small pot. Yearly practices can also be adjusted according to your fruit quality. If berries are small and dehydrated, you need more irrigation next year. For small-scale growers, because of the shallowness of most garden soils, you need to irrigate. Remember, less is better. Grapevines don't need copious amounts of water to survive!

SIMPLE YEARLY SIGNS FOR IRRIGATION PRACTICES

Simple Yearly Signs for Irrigation Practices

Fall/Winter

Root Zone should be sufficiently wet (12–15 inches) by rainfall or irrigation.

Spring: Mature vines don't need additional water unless root zone is completely dry (watch for signs!)

1. New shoots need to remain supple, soft, greenish-yellow, not hard, dry, or wilted

2. Grape flower clusters need to be fluffy, not dried out

3. Leaves need to be green, bright, crisp, not gray, dull, or limp

Early Summer

Irrigate when the vine leaves are not vibrant and healthy—wet soil to the depth of the roots.

Warm Regions

Approximately 1–8 irrigations (depending upon soil type)

Cooler Regions

Depending upon spring rainfall level, may not need irrigation

Mid to Late Summer

Once berries are established, do not irrigate (unless vines' leaves wilt or turn brown). Leaves should not drop until after harvest (nor should the fruit). If they threaten to, then you need to irrigate.

*Newly spring planted vines need soil kept moist for first 6 weeks.

ELEVEN

A WELL HALF FULL

*M*onsieur Eugene Boudreau, professional geologist and a polished-looking gentleman whose appearance led me to wonder if he had recently left England and was on his way to an African safari, showed up at my front door with clipboard in hand and carrying a thickly bound black leather book. "What's that?" I asked, wondering if I was going to assist him with the investigatory processes of my well situation.

"This here is my book of maps and rock formation data," he explained. "I'll investigate your land and look for places where water can be found, but hopefully you won't ever have to use this information." His exploration gear—khakis, hat, stick, and camera—suddenly made sense as I followed him while he strolled around my property, taking notes about water sources and rocks.

But I wondered what he was there for if I wasn't going to need his reports on where to dig a new well. "I'm not following, Mr. Boudreau, what exactly do you mean?"

"I'll explain later," he said. "But I want you to think about this statement while I check over your land: A successful well is one that has usable water flow coming from penetrable rock; in other words, the yield of your well depends upon the permeability of the rock that is present." I learned that my groundwater comes from local rainfall and that it percolates into the ground. The water is present in fractures and spaces in saturated rock that is below the water table; its movement is dependent upon how big the openings and spaces are within the rock. "Your well is 420 feet down with 5-foot plastic casing and 0.032-inch pipe perforations beginning at 240 feet," he said. It sounded way too technical and it was hard to imagine all those feet of pipe going through layers and layers of the earth. But I figured that his account of the facts would probably have some relevance later.

I didn't talk to Mr. Boudreau for six hours; I waited and thought about what he said. During the course of the day I saw him wandering through the bushes taking photos and poking his stick into the ground. All I could think of was that this all seemed so easy and why hadn't I hired him before now. He was competent and knew where to look, and when it came to finding water, that was exactly what I needed.

I needed water for my family and I wanted water for my grapes. The conservation practices we had so dutifully mastered weren't solving our water shortage. And before I found out that Monsieur Boudreau existed, our solid family structure started to collapse like a crumbling stone wall; our wretched emotional state was causing a rift in our family unit.

My family of optimists turned into a bunch of grumbling skeptics. We lost our comfortable family life together, we lost our fruitful crops, but most of all, we lost our faith. We just didn't believe that our sacrifices were worth it anymore, and we gave up on ever being able to feel the self-satisfaction that goes with beating the odds. Like defeated weather-beaten fishermen who battle the angry sea, we could no longer find any goodness in our ineffectual encounters with Mother Nature. We were ready to abandon our unproductive water conservation practices and forget we had ever attempted to farm this land.

Sometimes I wondered if the reason my well output dwindled from twenty gpm to nothing was because of all the times the water was allowed to escape. The fleeing, wasted water forced my well pump to continue working the well, sucking water for days, months, and even years while—on its way to the holding tank—it seeped out onto my mountainside. Hence, we burned through well pumps like a racecar driver might burn out engines. Worse yet, we wasted the water from our well.

And while the water continued to diminish, I spent many days secretly wishing to once again be the city person who turns on a faucet and always has water. On my trips to Sonoma—school drop-offs, sports, and socializing—I drove through suburban neighbor-hoods, envious of those cul-de-sac lifestyles. They had everything, I told myself, perfectly maintained front lawns, pizza delivery, man-icured parks (that someone else took care of), and most of all, unlimited water flowing from their faucets. Wouldn't it be nice to hear my neighbor's car door slam, or listen to the endless arguing of the elderly couple next door, or walk twenty feet from my doorstep to retrieve the mail? Some of the very things I had left the city for—concrete sidewalks, neighbors stopping by all the time, and lack of privacy—were becoming exactly what I missed the most.

I never told anyone about those feelings. Although my children, who were usually with me while I was driving through the suburban neighborhoods, figured out that my habitual, residential tours signified second thoughts about farming and country living, it was more about needing to know that there were other possibilities if I decided to abandon my dream of farming. Knowing that we could always escape to suburbia made it easier for us to go home at night. It's like the first time you jump off a diving board and you have no fear because someone is waiting in the water ready to catch you if you sink. You feel secure because there is a way out. We could go home to our farm with its fading water because we knew there was a place waiting to catch us if we really fell.

I finally quit those suburban car rides and reeled in on the reins of our wayward family wagon, and that's when things began to change for the better. When it came to the strength of the family unit, I realized that I was the heart that pumped the blood for sustenance; I was the water that kept the boat from scraping the rocks; I was the honey that kept the bees alive. "It's okay," I told my kids, "we'll find a way to make it work. We'll dig a giant hole and catch all the rainwater, or we'll buy water and pump it into our tank, or we'll ask the neighbors if we can buy water rights to their well." I felt that I had to step in and exude optimism to show my children how to be buoyant so they wouldn't become victims of what I was putting them through.

I told them it wasn't about their physical surroundings, it was about sticking together as a family, accepting the individual uniqueness of each other, and working through our problems together. We had to communicate during this hard period, to harmonize and make important decisions together, and help each other get through

the tough times. We became closer after that, learning how important we were to each other, and how to enjoy the company of one
another. When we no longer cared about the water was when things
changed. There were options, I found out, viable ways to attack our
problem that didn't necessarily mean digging a new well. That was
about the time I called on Monsieur Boudreau.

The news was good when he knocked on my front door, after
his day-long trek around my property. "I've found the likely spot for
water," he said, "but let's forget about that for now. Have you rede-
veloped your well since you've been living here?"

I wasn't sure what he was talking about, but I knew that we hadn't
done anything to our well except replace a few fuses in the circuit
breaker and put in a new pump. "I haven't touched it," I told him.

He scrunched up his face with a look of disdain. "Okay, I can
see were going to have to start from the beginning," he said. "There's
no need to panic about water at this point because you have many
things to do before we can actually determine if you need to dig a
new well."

He went on to tell me that there were no mysteries or hidden
secrets about water and that the location of groundwater within the
earth (which, unlike surface water, is the water that is underground)
should not be viewed as a mysterious act of God, nor should it be
discovered by a "water-witcher" with a witch stick.

"I'm ready to try anything." I went on to tell him that on numerous occasions the kids and I had tried doing rain dances that we had
learned from a tape we'd rented from the library. "But our dance
looked more like a combination of the Charleston and jitterbug with
a twist of tap dancing," I recalled.

"Did it work for you?" he asked, slightly amused.

"Nah, but I think we just haven't perfected it yet," I retorted.

He handed me a piece of paper with recommendations for redeveloping our existing well. "Follow those instructions. There are three easy steps, and if they don't help get more water for you, we'll talk about the next step—digging a new well," he said. He emphasized that by doing these redevelopment processes I could encourage yield, aide with the operating efficiency of the well, and improve the overall life of my well.

"I hope this works," I muttered as he drove away.

✳ ✳ ✳

The list laid out three to-do items for redeveloping my existing well:

1. Take a videotaped log of the well to check for areas of perforations in the pipes.
2. Remove encrustations by treating well with hydroxyacetic acid (glycolic acid)—an organic acid that is a bactericide and dissolves iron deposits and mineral scales. (You need a specialist to do this.)
3. After acid treatment, hire jetting specialist to high-speed jet well using air and water. This agitates and cleans out well pipe perforations by blowing out debris and encrustations that have become blocked over time.

✳ ✳ ✳

It seemed too good to be true; there had to be a catch. Three easy steps and we'd be on our way to hot baths and irrigated grapevines. I'll never forget the day I spent sitting in a giant, white van parked in the middle of my vineyard watching the inside of my well casing on a television screen. The two women in charge of the filming seemed proficient enough, and once they'd actually gotten the mammoth vehicle through the vineyard—which lasted the better part of the morning and resulted in quite a bit of vegetation removal—things ran smoothly.

"The oak trees needed pruning anyway," I told them. "Don't worry about the brush piles; we'll chop them up next time the tractor makes a pass through the vineyard." The van was big, and I didn't want to make them feel bad. I was just relieved that the vines were still standing.

The goal of the video was to take pictures of the inside of our well so we could figure out where our pipe perforations were, and determine if they were blocked.

"Looks pretty darn clean in there," they told me. I saw a long, dark piece of something that had another object attached to it.

"What about that black thing?" I asked, hoping I had found some giant problem that would offer answers and allow a quick solution for fixing the well.

"Oh, that's just a stick with a frog attached to it," one woman said. It seemed like I couldn't get away from the frogs; they loved my yard, they loved my vineyard, and they loved my well.

It took hours to videotape four hundred feet of piping, and we saw many frogs. By the end of the day, the camera women weren't sure about the situation of the perforations and told me that the owner of the company would have to review the tape before any determinations could be made.

"Do you have even a vague idea?" I begged, "I really just need to know." I'd had enough of waiting, and another week of wondering seemed like an eternity, especially knowing my children would start in with their nagging.

Dude was the first to ask. "Mom!" he screamed, as he came bursting through the front door, "What's the verdict, can they fix it?"

I tried to outmaneuver him and hide upstairs, not wanting to tell him that we'd need to wait a week for the results, but then I saw Joy coming down the road toward me. She was stopped near the vineyard, and I could see her looking at the piles of oak tree debris that were laying in between vineyard rows. "Mom, why are there mounds of tree limbs all over the vineyard?" she asked. Nothing slipped by this family, and I knew there'd be lots of explaining to do at the dinner table that night.

Sure enough, the conversation at the dinner table revolved around what I knew. The problem was that I wouldn't know anything for a whole week. But I certainly didn't tell them that I knew about the wild life living in the well, knowing they would forever think about all those frogs every time they turned on a faucet.

The judgment from the film screening was ambiguous, but I was told that there was hope for more water and to go ahead with the next step of redeveloping the well—the glycolic clean-out. I called Gil and the well people began the process of breaking down the encrustations on the well casing. I watched as they put glycolic acid into the well, interrogating them about the process. The acid would remain in the well for twenty-four hours and then be neutralized and pumped out. Gil explained to me that doing this process would not only clean out the perforations in the well pipe casings, but it would also purify the water.

"Purifying our well water was once important to us," I said.

"It still should be for anyone with a well," he replied.

His comment took me back to a time a while back when we had all been very sick. Months passed as we seemed to pass the stomach flu between us. I finally figured out that the stomach ailments we were experiencing were not from the flu, however. Instead, there was a serious problem with the potability of what we were consuming. You are what you eat, and in this case we were what we drank—parasite-ridden and unhealthy. Everyone had the same intestinal problem except Bubba the dog. He drank only bottled water and ate special dog food that didn't require any use of water from the well.

"Please help us!" I screamed into my phone. "My dog ate the parasite medicine I'm supposed to be giving my children. What should I do?" I was wondering how I was going to administer mouth-to-mouth to the long, hairy snout of my bad-breathed wire-haired dachshund. "First of all, ma'am, what exactly did your dog eat?" the Poison Control phone operator calmly questioned.

"He ate the flagyl and yodoxin that I laid out for my three children," I replied, trying to mask my fear. (He'd climbed on a chair and lapped up the sugar-coated pills I'd carefully placed for each child on the kitchen table.) I'd done this each morning for nearly a week without any problems or canine thievery from Bubba.

"Is this a joke? You mean to tell me your dachshund ate 'yo dachshund'?" he asked. "I get it."

"Look, whatever your name is, this is not a joke," I pleaded.

"What should I do?" I was worried that the drugs would be toxic to the dog and especially in a dosage that was tripled.

"Ma'am, we don't specialize in house pets," he said. "I can't honestly say."

We all took turns watching Bubba sleep soundly through the night. By the next morning there were no signs of any toxicity, and I continued to treat my children with the parasite medicine by placing the tablets directly on each of their tongues when Bubba wasn't looking.

"So, you're telling me that this acid treatment will take care of the problem of bacteria in the well? Because we are about due for another water test." It had been a year since our illnesses and it was time to check the water again. "Yup, you'll be set for another year," Gil told me. I had learned the hard way that wells need to be checked for bacteria, and whatever else might go wrong down there, at least once a year—even if you aren't drinking the water. Particles left on food from washing your vegetables and cooking pasta is all it takes to infect the human intestine.

After the acid treatment, and before the jetting was done, Grace brought home two ducklings with a note taped to their wings reading: "Don't bring back unless on a silver platter with orange sauce." She and two of her high school friends had bought the ducklings several weeks prior from a person selling them on the street in Sonoma. They had decided to raise them "together," each of them taking the two ducklings for a couple of weeks at a time, hiding them so that none of the parents could object. This was not a practical idea since the birds made noise all night long, pooped incessantly, and grew like weeds. I thought the parent who'd sent the note to be rather harsh until we had the birds for a couple of days and I found out for myself what a messy nuisance they were. The attached note even brought a small smile to my face after I was forced to scrub down Grace's splattered bedroom wall and drain the black bathtub water they used for their daily swims.

In the process of caring for those ducks, though, I learned something about my water. I already knew that we had hard water, but I certainly didn't think that having hard water would mean that I could actually see the manganese, iron, and small portions of bacteria from nature floating in it, nor did I think I was bathing in liquid that looked like murky pond water. Our water was perfect for the ducks because it reminded them of their native habitat: black, gritty, and smelly. There were pieces of rock—probably remnants from the acid clean-out—and there were black, sandy chunks laying on the floor of the white porcelain tub. This went way beyond hard water. I was told not to worry about this because *if* the cleaning out of the perforations were successful, then the water would probably be less hard. *If* didn't seem very encouraging to me.

The jetting process was completed and Mr. Boudreau's steps for well redevelopment were accomplished. We held our tongues and didn't gloat about our newfound knowledge for well redevelopment. No one I knew had ever talked about these techniques, but I didn't want to go around making statements that it really worked until I actually had our results. It would be like announcing my winnings from a horse race that hadn't taken place yet.

The clean-smelling, remnant-free water flowed through our faucets, and it gushed from our irrigation equipment. But still, we waited, fearing we would jinx our good fortune. One morning I felt compelled to watch the water dowsing my garden. I looked out my bedroom window, and much to my surprise, I saw water spraying and great clouds of steam rising from the ground floating twenty feet in the air.

"Chuck," I yelled into him as he was taking his morning shower, "were you messing with the outdoor fireplace last night?" I felt certain that he had used some strange wood to burn a fire and that it had smoked and smoldered all night.

"What are you talking about?" He stepped out of the shower and came to the window. We both stood there speechless.

In the process of well development we had either hit, exposed, unshrouded, or uncovered a hot springs. From then on the Moulton residence could be listed in the directory under the "spa" section. When I called Gil to inquire about how this could have happened, I heard him laughing on the other end of the receiver. "Paula, you are only a quarter of a mile from Morton's Warm Springs and that whole mountain is filled with mineral hot springs and has been for hundreds of years. Why do you think the Native Americans loved that area so much?" he joked. I guess he had a point.

Suddenly we had lots and lots of water—steaming water—all without having had to dig a new well. And ... having a spring underground might just be a good thing for my grapevines that weren't getting any aboveground water.

Our dances to the water gods must have worked below ground instead of aboveground. Who am I to question where the water arrives from? Just as long as it finds its way to the roots of my vines. Its entrance below ground has allowed me to continue dry farming and my vines are happy, my fruit is intense, and my desire to manage and conserve water has been a success.

HARD WATER AND HOW TO TREAT IT

Signs To Watch For

- Iron causes orange stains to clothing and plumbing fixtures and corrodes pipes
- Maganese produces gritty, black deposits in water, stains the plumbing fixtures, and corrodes pipes
- Sulfur bacteria and hydrogen-sulfide give water a rotten egg smell and taste

How To Treat Hard Water

All of these problems can be alleviated by chlorination, water softening (adding salt), and filtration. Water testing companies can run a complete analysis that give breakdowns and acceptable ranges for homeowners and grape-growers.

BASIC YEARLY TIPS FOR MAINTAINING HEALTHY, PRODUCTIVE WELLS

1. Chemical levels of water should be tested every 3–5 years (water-testing companies do this)

2. Bacteria levels of water should be tested once a year (especially if you drink the well water)

3. If contaminated, disinfect well following specifications of your water company (we use household bleach)

4. Every couple of years check the pumping rate by doing a test (my well went from 20 gpm to 8 gpm in 10 years, but after redevelopment the levels went up again)

5. Measure water depth level in spring and fall of each year by attaching a weight to a string and lowering the line into the well until it hits water (make note of this point)

6. Pull up line and record distance between top of line to weight (if levels continue to drop with each season, begin redevelopment process)

7. Redevelop well—videotape the well casings to locate perforations, acid treat, and swab or jet clean

TWELVE

IN VINES WE TRUST

I was looking through a viticulture publication when I spotted a Help Wanted ad that read: Biodynamic Farmer Wanted. The blurb under the heading described the job as a "stunning opportunity for dedicated farmers to participate in healing agricultural approaches and spiritual mending." *Hmph,* I thought, *I could surely use that.* "But I certainly don't need another job," I said out loud, hoping to catch my drifting attention and turn my wandering thoughts back to figuring out how to change my hot water—from our new mineral hot spa—into cold water. And still I was drawn to what I read. I kept on scanning the article, looking for things about farming that I could understand. My biggest hope for reading on was to discover that someone else had uncovered all the brilliant truths about agronomy, and I would no longer need to keep searching; instead, I could just follow behind in their footsteps. I didn't find that, but I became so intrigued by the ad that I made the telephone call to the listed phone number. Pretending to be an applicant who might be interested in the job, I asked them specifics about the position, questioning them about what the biodynamic processes entailed, inquiring about how this farming technique could possibly mend my soul and heal my spirit, toying with the possibility of trying yet another farming path. It seemed to me that there were still so many things to learn about farming, and just when I thought I might be catching up with all the techniques and processes, something new popped up in front of me. But like a child who wants to try the newest sweet in the candy store, I've always got to take a stab at trying the new product—gorge myself with its many flavors and bellyache my way through its consumption.

I never got the name of the person I talked to, nor did I apply for the job they were trying to fill. I did, however, get enough information to wet my curiosity, encourage more investigation, and figure out that these farming techniques aren't far from where I ultimately wanted to be. The person on the other end of the phone— probably the writer of the farming ad—began his soliloquy by telling me that the Greek word biodynamic means *bio* for life and *dynamic* for energy, which in farming, he said, translates into using the forces of nature to grow crops. That didn't seem so out-of-the-ordinary to me, a little vague and a bit broad maybe, but nothing so extreme that I'd need a dictionary to translate. "Can you be a little more specific about how you expect your employee to approach this farming style?" I asked, hoping he'd tell me more about this type of farming. It sounded so intriguing.

"Sure," he said, "biodynamic farming eliminates all use of synthetic fertilizers and chemicals by replacing them with composts, cover crops, herbal remedies, and quartz sprays, and incorporates energy balancing techniques that use the earth cycles to encourage healthy soils and plants. We believe that the rhythms of the local environment and the universe—the actions of the moon, sun, planets, and stars—contribute to the normal life cycles of plants on earth." He followed his descriptions by informing me that "in Australia, there are over a million and a quarter acres of crops grown using biodynamic farming techniques."

When I hung up the phone I was pleased that I was already composting, cover cropping, and encouraging microorganism populations, but I wondered how I could find out more about the herbal remedies, sprays, and using the cycles of the earth to grow grapes. I learned that biodynamic farming originated in the early 1900s by a doctor named Rudolph Steiner. Although Steiner was trained in natural sciences, he formulated biodynamic farming principles from a broad array of concepts—treatises of famous philosophers like Aristotle and Goethe, gardens from medieval times, Christian mystics, alchemy, holistic health, herbalism, and common folk wisdom. He believed that farmers must practice a spiritual understanding of the powerful energy of nature in order to grow healthy, thriving plants, and that objective, quantitative theories, although they play a part in farming, must not be accepted as the whole truth. But I was even more inspired by his philosophic discussions about healing the mind and the body, and about why the farmers who use this technique are so driven by doctrines from wise thinkers like Plato and Aristotle. I'd spent years in college studying their teachings, and although I became well versed in many of these ideas, they didn't hold much practicality for me. I guess it's that old truism that sometimes things make sense long after the fact. I'd experienced this so many times in my life already, but chose to ignore it. Farming, Steiner believed, should concern itself with spiritual discernment as well as scientific understanding. The answers to questions like, how do I feel when I am able to watch my plants grow? and what insight have I gained from the blissful effects of a contented garden? and what is it about this process that makes me so happy? aren't as important as the questions themselves.

The man on the phone also said that using manmade chemicals and discouraging the natural processes of healthy soil can actually force plants into winter dormancy—when it's not winter! I'd seen this happen on my own farm when my soil turned to concrete from all the chemicals we'd used to kill off the weeds (which also killed all the living organisms within the soil). Worst of all, I'd seen the results of dead soil when, in the summer, my fruit had dropped off the vine long before harvest, and the vines' leaves shriveled up and floated away long before winter. Before I switched to organic farm-ing, I saw the catastrophic results of dead soil: grapevines that didn't know what season it was, lack of fruit, and feelings of failure that came from the upsetting results. (These frustrations had certainly NOT produced feelings of well being.)

"Nuts," Chuck said when I told him about how enthralling bio-dynamic farming seemed, "you're just plain out of your mind." I could tell this was going to be another one of our battles, akin to our lavender conflicts, and like my "scatterbrained," as he called it, insis-tence that we must stop spraying chemicals on the vines. Chuck was happy following the established rules for growing grapes; he wanted to follow the mainstream techniques for farming. I wanted none of it. I finally just hired Phil Coturri, the guru of organics, and flaunted Phil's accomplishments. This helped my cause enormously. How could he argue with a reputable, well-known male farmer? I'd hired Phil years ago when I first discovered that my soil was dead. He helped me set up composting and cover cropping regimes, and I took the old traditions of farming away so slowly that Chuck didn't notice—like a mother weaning her child off the breast. Phil helped me get started, and he had the equipment and knowledge for composting and cover cropping in the fall, spot burning the weeds with propane in the spring, and disking the dissipated cover crop in the summer to create mulch that captured the important moisture of the land. When Chuck realized how healthy the vines were becoming, I told him the truth. I knew not to hit him head on with vagaries and risks; I knew that he would want scientific data and cold, hard facts. There were no such things in farming; I could only give him the proof once it had occurred on our land—long after I'd started the process without his support.

The finer details of biodynamic farming were explained to me by Mike Benziger from the Benziger Family Winery in Glen Ellen. He runs an innovative, successful vineyard and believes in preservation of the land and conservation of its resources. Benziger Winery is just minutes from me as the crow flies, and I consider it a great privilege to be so close to a renowned winery that practices progressive and inspirational farming principles. Mike greeted me by describing the winery's basic beliefs on grape-growing and winemaking. "Our central goal," he said, "is to create an individually unique ecosystem which can achieve in the flavors and textures of the grape and wine a complete expression of the character and personality of a particular plot of land. This approach is as self-sufficient and sustainable as possible with respect to the cycle of the materials it requires."

I learned that they have been farming their many acres of vineyards for five years using this process, and they are experts on the techniques and philosophies of this type of vineyard management. Mike let me snoop around his biodynamic vineyards and filled me in on certain yearly rituals that I'd never heard of before. I'd never really thought much about the fact that the positive benefits of the atmosphere—heat, air, and light—could actually be encouraged and directed to produce healthier trees, plants, and crops. He explained that along with composting, cover cropping, and spot burning—to remove unwanted weeds from growing under the grapevines—one can purchase things like powdered quartz crystals to reinforce deficit or altered sources of light when the vines are not getting enough, or nettle infusions to stimulate the flow of sap in the grapevine in years of drought or low rainfall. There are many different treatments and most of them can be mixed in with compost, depending upon what is needed in a given year.

"How would I know what treatments my vines needed and where would I find such treatments?" I asked him, thinking the process sounded rather complicated. He told me that ideally the different sprays and composts should be produced from elements that are specific to where the grapevines are being grown, and they should be used at times when the universal rhythms of the solar system can aide in the plants uptake, stimulate the healthy activity within soil, and vitalize the plant. This is exactly where French winemaker Nicolas Joly's concept of "everyone needs a cow" comes into play, and the naturally healthy partnership between animals and land that are significant to the process of biodynamic farming. In order for the grapevines to remain healthy and able to fend off the negative influences of the environment—including pests and disease—the sprays and composts, in conjunction with cosmic forces of energy and nature, must help create and foster healthy soils that in turn produce robust, well-balanced plants. Mike followed this by sharing with me the numerous biodynamic farming associations all over the United States that direct farmers with the what, when, and where of this process. "In other words," I summarized from all I had heard, "we must trust that our vines, their soil, and the environment and the universe around them have everything that's needed to maintain and continue the plants health."

After my meeting with Benziger, I went away understanding that grape-growers and winemakers practicing biodynamic farming go beyond just using certain techniques to promote the health of nature; it is not just a holistic approach that takes into account all aspects of grapevine growth—soil, vines, and the unseen energies and forces of nature that influence their life. It also takes into account the beliefs that fruit produced from this type of farming can produce outstanding wines that are unique to the specific place they are grown in. I think biodynamic farmers are not just farmers; they are philosophers who treat the growing of crops from an intellectual and spiritual as well as scientific point of view. The wines become a reflection of their vineyard site—the soil and the climate—with exceptional flavors that are characteristic of the interaction between the land and the universe on that specific site.

* * *

The biodynamic concepts reminded me of a time when I went on a field trip with Joy and her fourth grade class. We visited a museum that was located on a site where Native Americans once lived. Our tour was given by a man who seemed to know everything about that actual area and about how the people lived on that particular spot. One of the most fascinating parts of the tour was his description of how they treated themselves when they got poison oak. (I always pay attention when there are discussions of this, since I've been terrorized with the rash more times than I care to remember.) We were told that the inhabitants, afflicted with the rash, went to the place where the poison oak was and dug up the plants that were growing next to it, making a salve from their components. It was their belief that any plant surviving near the rash-inducing bush would be able to withstand the toxic consequences of the poison oak plant and provide the best source to treat its effects.

When I first began growing grapes, I was convinced that my job as farmer was to control my vineyard's environment by removing all unwanted weeds, animals, insects, and disease using manmade fertilizers, insecticides, herbicides, and pesticides, thinking this would produce healthy vines that would give me glowing, sweet-tasting crops. Like creating a beautiful meal with all the ingredients carefully organized and calculated, I held true to the doctrine that I was there to organize and clean up the land—no nasty smells, no dusty paths, no leaves out-of-place, no animal remnants. Then I would have perfect fruit and award-winning wine. I've since learned that it's not about keeping nature manicured, it's about encouraging

SOME SIMPLE BIODYNAMIC PRINCIPLES

1. No use of hormones, antibiotics, synthesized fertilizers, fungicides, herbicides, or pesticides

2. Use compost, manure, green manure, cover crops, crop rotations, quartz sprays, and applications of biodynamic compost preparations in order to maintain a healthy, fertile crop

3. Weeds are controlled by spot burning or other natural ways, such as grazing cows

4. Pests are controlled by maintaining a balanced farm ecosystem and managing of the vineyard area crop rotation, crop diversification, and canopy management

5. Maintaining balanced ecosystem (to manage pests) through soil management, biodynamic sprays, canopy management, irrigation, and crop rotating

6. Sources used should come from land where crops are grown with the exception of certain biodynamic preparations for compost transformation, herbal remedies, and sprays

For more information contact the Biodynamic Farming and Gardening Association, Inc. at http://www.biodynamics.com.

Summer

Wine makes daily living easier, less hurried, with
fewer tensions and more tolerance.
—Benjamin Franklin

SUMMER IN PARIS

2012

There is nothing better than red wine and pizza—if you're in Italy, of course. But I actually learn this in Paris at Le Cordon Bleu. Pizza and red wine are not a traditionally accepted pairing in France because, according to the French, pizza is not a high-quality food and would be better paired with beer. Even further from French traditions are the habits of the Chinese students in my class: They tell me that they mix Coca-Cola with Bordeaux red wine and absolutely love the combination when served with any type of Asian food. So really, what is all the hoopla about food and wine pairing, and is it real or merely a standard of tradition and enforced rules that no longer make sense?

This summer, I am a sommelier at Citrus Etoile, a swanky restaurant in the 8th arrondissement in Paris just blocks from the Champs Elysees. My job is to help my guests with their food and wine pairings, but I must do this the traditional French way, which means no pairings of pizza and red wine. I find myself in yet one more situation in France that pushes me to my limits in my knowledge of food and wine.

The restaurant was opened in 2005 when Chef Giles Epie, the youngest chef to receive a Michelin star (at age twenty-two), embarked on an innovative cuisine adventure after spending many years abroad in Southern California as a chef at L'Orangerie. He combines French, Mediteranean, and Californian cuisine to create healthy gastronomic magic. I am here on an internship that will afford me hands-on experience with a renowned French chef and curious international foodies who come to experience cuisine that is seasonal and non-traditional and that boasts less butter and cream.

The wine cave, located behind a closed sliding glass door, is where we set up wine, prepare mixed drinks, and make sure that the cellar is properly stocked with the wines on the menu. During my first few days of work, I ask David, the head sommelier and my boss, why there aren't any California wines on this international restaurant menu. "Because no one would buy them, and the traditional French wanted only old-world style wines and not new-world style American wines," he says. "It is a shame, but we can't sell them."

My favorite order to take is a *coup de Champagne* (glass of Champagne). The key word here is "glass," which means that I don't have to set up my ice bucket and actually open the Champagne tableside. This is a great relief because my Champagne opening skills are lacking. "No noise, no shaking of the bottle, and certainly no explosion," Monsieur Ramage had always said, "because while you are serving the guests you will run a great risk of not only splattering Champagne all over them but possibly seriously injuring someone with a flying cork, not to mention wasting this precious liquid."

"*Bonjour, Mesdames et Monsieurs*," I say, handing the women, oldest to youngest, and then the men their menus. "Can I bring you a *coup de Champagne*?" This table is all mine for today, and I will assist them in picking their entire meal from start to finish. Beginning a formal meal with a glass of Champagne is customary in France and a ritual that I like because it gives me time while they sip to size them up and figure out what I think they might like to eat and drink. I will then be ready to determine their wine pairing, creating a perfect meal for them once they have completed their Champagne.

Why can't we pair any food with any wine and always have an outrageous meal? Our goal is to enhance the flavor of food with wine and turn neither the food nor the wine into an unpalatable beast in our mouths, and there is such a dramatic range of flavors out there that truthfully, combining any food with any wine might bring us disaster. I like to make the connection between the seven-minute-abs concept and random food and wine pairing. If we try to take shortcuts, we might end up with flabby abs, like our seven-minute folks, and I might end up with angry and unhappy restaurant guests leaving after barely touching their food or wine simply because I recommended an inedible pairing. And that would cost me my internship and a failing grade.

I use the KISS rule, or Keep It Simple Stupid rule, when it comes to food and wine pairing. I believe that overthinking food and wine pairing is dangerous if not ridiculous. I have two simple options when it comes to pairing: I can complement my food with my wine and harmonize the flavors, or I can contrast my food and wine and emphasize the differences. Whether I choose to emphasize similarities or differences, I still aim to enhance both my food and my wine.

A creamy white sauce served over pasta and a nice Sauvignon Blanc would pair well because the acidity of the wine contrasts with the smooth, creaminess of the sauce. A heavy beef stew with lots of pepper and bay leaves would complement a peppery, earthy red wine like a Cabernet Sauvignon because the bold aromas and flavors of the wine are similar to the strong and spicy ingredients in the stew.

I also like to use the seasons to help me draw conclusions about what wine to serve with meals, since my food is dictated so much by weather and the seasons. On a hot summer day would you be more likely to reach for a bold, tannic red wine or a crisp, fruity white wine? On the flipside, which sounds more appealing on a wintry night in February: a luscious, spicy red wine or a crisp, dry white wine? Our food choices center around the seasons just as much as our wine choices. On a steamy summer day, I would certainly prefer poached salmon and sun-ripened peach compote with an acidic, or even fruity white wine rather than a beef bourguignon and mashed potatoes with a hearty Cabernet Sauvignon. But give me that beef bourguignon and hearty Cabernet on a cool wintry night, and I am completely content.

Determining whether a wine is tannic or acidic can also help when it comes to pairing. Tannins in wine help cut the fat in food, and they are more prevalent in red wine than in white wine. Therefore, rich and fatty sauces and meats with higher fat content generally pair well with red wines. When we are enjoying these types of dishes, our tongues become coated in fat, and the tannins from the red wine break down the fat accumulated in our mouths, allowing us to not only enjoy the wine but also cleanse our palate for the next bite. Red wines that are specifically high in tannins are Cabernet Sauvignon, Syrah, Sangiovese, Zinfandel, and sometimes Merlot.

Tannins are generally low in white wine. When it comes to choosing white wine, remember that they are high in acidity, which allows them to pair well with foods that are also high in acidity, such as fish in lemon sauce and salad with acidic dressings. They also pair well with foods that are very low in acid, such as many seafood dishes, light cream sauces, and special cheeses. Some acidic white wines are Sauvignon Blanc, Riesling, Chenin Blanc, and Chardonnay.

When it comes to Asian food, Thai food, and Indian food, the best pairing options seem to be sweeter white wines and fruitier red wines, steering away from highly acidic or highly tannic wines, because these types of foods tend to be sweet. A sweet white wine like a Gewürztraminer, Semillon, Muscat, Viognier, or sweet Riesling, or a fruiter red wine like Zinfandel, Merlot, or Pinot Noir will complement the sweetness of these foods, whereas an acidic white wine might taste sour, and a tannic red wine might taste astringent and bitter.

Just like many learned things, once you become proficient with the basics, you can branch out and become a little more adventurous. You can do this by creating links to the wine you plan to serve in your food recipes. For instance, if you're serving a Pinot Noir, you could add black cherry, sage, or rose petals to a sauce to mimic the characteristics of that particular wine. Or you might prepare a passion fruit granita to place atop raw oysters and then serve an unoaked Chardonnay that mimics those tropical fruit flavors. The options become endless once you can escape the shackles of fear and take the grand leap of faith in favor of fun and adventure with food and wine. The goal is to have your food and wine work together without overshadowing one another. And the bottom line is to have fun and drink what you like.

After working for a month at Citrus Etoile and recommending nothing but traditional pairings, I couldn't wait to get home and test out my pairing knowledge with everyday meals. After some experimenting, I put together my own simple wine guide for typical American dishes, and it might help you get started when you begin choosing wines for yourself.

Wine Guide for Typical American Dishes

Asian Food: Gewurztraminer, Pinot Noir, Riesling, Semillon, Zinfandel

Brownies: Cabernet Sauvignon, Merlot, Syrah

Caesar Salad: Dry Riesling, Sauvignon Blanc

Chicken: Beaujolais, Chardonnay, Pinot Noir, Riesling, Rioja

Chocolate Chip Cookies: Champagne, Merlot

Hamburgers: Merlot, Rose, Syrah

Indian Food: Gewürztraminer, Pinot Noir, Riesling, Semillon, Zinfandel

Lasagne (red sauce): Chianti, Merlot, Zinfandel

Lasagne (white sauce): Gavi

Lamb: Bordeaux Blend, Cabernet Sauvignon, Merlot

Macaroni and Cheese: Chardonnay, Rioja, Sauvignon Blanc

Mexican Food: Riesling, Rose, Sauvignon Blanc

Omelet: Chardonnay, Champagne, Chenin Blanc, Sauvignon Blanc

Pasta (red sauce): Chianti, Pinot Grigio, Zinfandel

Pasta (white sauce): Chardonnay, Pinot Grigio

Pizza: Bordeaux, Merlot, Sauvignon Blanc, Syrah

Salmon: Chardonnay, Pinot Noir, Sauvignon Blanc

Seafood: Chardonnay, Riesling, Sauvignon Blanc

Shellfish: Chardonnay, Riesling, Sauvignon Blanc

Steak and Potatoes: Bordeaux, Cabernet Sauvignon, Merlot, Syrah

Thai Food: Gewurztraminer, Pinot Noir, sweet Riesling,
Semillon, Zinfandel
Turkey (Dark Meat): Merlot
Turkey (Light Meat): Chardonnay, Pinot Noir, Viognier
White Fish: Chardonnay, Viognier

* * *

It is my last day of class in late May, and at the bottom of my spiral-bound notebook I write a list titled, "The Gifts I Want":

1. Infrared thermometer (Raytek)
2. Battery-operated cork opener
3. Temperature-controlled wine cellar (preferably with a
   pretty water fountain—small)

I pause and think for a moment, and below my list I write in capital letters, BUT REALLY, ALL I WANT IS TO GO HOME!

Exams begin in ten days. The door of Le Cordon Bleu shuts behind me, and I breathe in the chilly May air of Paris. The fact that I have spent ten months alone in France without my fiancé and children seems unreal and more like a dream to me. I smile and laugh to myself because I am nearly done, and I feel an overwhelming sense of accomplishment, and more importantly, an astounding new hope for my future.

THIRTEEN

SOMEWHERE OVER THE VINEYARD

*W*hen summer finally arrives, I calmly take in a big whiff of warm air and sigh as I let it out. Summer is the interlude when the sun parches the land and the atmosphere is motionless; it's a time to relax and let the yellow fireball in the sky melt away all the past year's darkness. Gratitude penetrates this familiar and timely bit of serenity making this season a formidable memory awakened with each new year. I embrace its quenching tranquility by stroking the unflurried effects with reposeful thought and settled breaths.

"I think you like summertime the best," Chuck says.

"Why do you say so?" I ask him.

"Because it's harvest time and because you can invent new recipes with your out-of-control lavender," he jokes. He's right that I never use recipes to cook with, that I prefer to throw things together and watch what happens, that I don't make pastries or sweets because they flop with my uncalculated measurements, and that friends don't dare ask me for recipes because I don't have any. Chances are good that if you like one of my meals you'd better remember it because I'll never be able to recreate it the same way.

"I do love it, but I'm not sure that I like summer best," I tell Chuck, as I'm standing in our kitchen sipping Jewel Viognier, pounding abalone, and preparing bay scallops in olive oil and sweet vermouth for our seafood tacos with grilled onions and tomatillo salsa. "I can't decide which season I like the most in the Sonoma wine country. They are all so different."

✳ ✳ ✳

"Where the hell is summer?" I ask him, wondering if I'm breaking my own traditions by consuming what I think should be an appropriate wine and food for summer—even if there are no signs of it. It's nearly June of 2003 and I'm still waiting for my moments of peace; I'm still waiting for the baking heat of the sun; I'm still waiting for unhurried thinking; I'm still waiting to experience the windless, stormless days of summertime; and I'm still waiting for bloom to begin. I'm looking somewhere over the rainbow trying to see the next season coming. But the frogs are still croaking—which means frog mating season isn't over and neither is bud break—and until they stop producing their overpowering subpoenas, bloom won't happen. History has taught me this, and as frustrating as it is, there's nothing I can do about it.

In Sonoma wine country, summer normally starts in early May—but not this year. I had a discussion about the idiosyncrasies of summer at my Ravenswood grape-growers' luncheon in mid-May. All the growers were complaining about how strange the weather has been this year, and about how much disruption it will cause to the grapevines. Translation: There will be loss of crop if the weather doesn't warm up during bloom, and more loss of crop if the fruit is not ready by the end of summer and the fall rains come before harvest. Cold weather will mean bloom shatter, and rainfall before harvest will mean rotted grapes that won't ripen—a melancholy scenario.

During the grape-growers' discussion on the subject of miserable weather, and while we feasted on savory beet, bean, and prawn salad, seared tri-tip with couscous, creamy strawberry shortcake and, of course, copious amounts of delectable Ravenswood wines, including Icon, their Rhone-style wine, Sangiacomo Chardonnay, and Pickberry Cabernet Sauvignon, Don Williams and Diane Kenworthy soothed the audience of overindulged farmers. The previous year, along with superb food, their calmative jargon centered around the fluctuating wine markets and the volatile economy. This year, along with the marvelous food, their talk danced around weather and the clever twists of Mother Nature. They focused on remaining optimistic and the necessity for everyone to keep a hopeful attitude. I wondered about the viability of optimism for me. Optimism, as I know it in philosophic terms, means viewing the world as constantly improving, as a place where good rises above evil. I can't seem to fathom this after having lived through some rough years of grapevine hardships: my crop dropping to the ground before harvest, forced dry farming without a weaning program, animals feasting on my fruit, dead soil, and now the horrific realization that this year the weather might bruise and beat my crop. But I know that in this business I must believe in positive outcomes no matter what my circumstances.

The epiphany hits me later, after I leave my yearly Ravenswood meeting. That's it, I tell myself, as I hear Don and Diane's voices in the back of my mind telling the growers how much the winery appreciates them, and how much our unique personalities add to the character of Ravenswood wine. Yes, I say to myself, it's not about producing the biggest crop, it's about carrying on the tradition of wine under the assumption that wine is composed of a conglomeration of many different personalities blended together as one. I play a very small role; nonetheless, I present a certain disposition to the finality of the wine. For the moment, this satisfies my desire to continue as a grape-grower. I'm happy believing that the wine is interesting and fruitful because it is a mixture of me and the particularity of my vineyard. (This perspective is from the vantage point of a farmer; winemakers also play a HUGE role in making wine come alive with the complex diversity of characters—grapes and grape-growers.)

Ten years ago, I started out as a raw, inexperienced landowner who followed the accepted doctrines for vineyard management: In the fall I left the vines alone; when winter rolled around I pruned them according to textbook rules; in the spring I sprayed the hell out of them with herbicides and insecticides (and if they looked a little weepy or tattered I synthetically fertilized them); in the summer I sprayed them again if I saw a bug or a weed, and then I picked their fruit. It really wasn't until I failed, and failed again, and failed again, that I realized I had to be doing something wrong.

I remembered a time about five years ago when I first began doubting these very procedures. Ironically, it was at this exact moment that I was asked to speak about grape-growing and wine-making at a local middle school. Let's see, I thought to myself, how can I entertain a bunch of pre-adolescents on a subject they may find rather boring? I'd already found out from my own children that this was a tiresome subject and one that would be uninteresting—no matter how I presented it. I decided to present the information using a game that I had carefully crafted a few evenings before the talk. Little did I know that the game would do more than just teach them about grape-growing; it would also teach me many more things about the importance of using the seasons to farm, and about the importance of encouraging the natural processes of nature. This helped me continue to look for alternatives to my faltering vineyard procedures.

While the students listened to my description of a year in the life of a grapevine, I asked them to close their eyes and visualize the characteristics of each season: colors, smells, and sounds. I wanted them to think about these features so they would understand how active a role the seasons play in the process of agriculture, realize their own close connection with nature and how much their lives exist in harmony with the seasons in a year, and understand that the yearly traditions of the seasons can make them feel connected with their past and help them move toward their future.

We started with the kids' descriptions of how fall made them feel. One kid blurted out, "I hate fall because school starts, but I feel excited too, because trick-or-treating is close." I quickly described what a grapevine does in the fall. The leaves drop to the ground leaving a pungent, earthy smell floating through the air. The odor comes from the decomposition process—bacteria and worms in the ground eating through the structure of the leaves.

"Yeah," another student exclaimed. "It's kind of like the calm before the storm; you feel energized by fall and at the same time you realize that the slowness of winter is close." I wasn't sure if they were listening to me, but I kept on with my spiel.

"Yes," I said, "just like how the fall grapevine, in preparation for winter, might absorb large quantities of decomposed nutrients, you guys consume massive quantities of Halloween candy, and just like the grapevine, after it bulks up, begins turning its energy inward ready to shut down for the winter, you guys turn off your brains just in time for Thanksgiving vacation."

"Yeah!" they said in unison, letting on that they understood exactly what I was saying.

"And," I said, "in winter, while the vine is dormant and resting, the soil remains alive with microorganisms that continue working to break down available nutrients that the vine will use when spring-time arrives." I told them that the microorganisms in the soil also help produce substances that increase soil aeration, water retention, and neutralize pH. And I told them that in late winter, weeds and wildflowers begin a self-reseeding process as they germinate and regenerate from seeds dropped to the ground after the previous growing season.

"When spring arrives and the grapevine begins a period of breathtaking growth, aided by the available nutrients stored in the winter soil, the energy of the vine is directed outward," I said. "The fruit begins maturation, the wildflowers and weeds begin dying off, dropping their leaves and flowers onto the ground, decomposing and generating more nutrients for the vines' fruit development."

"And finally," I concluded, "the summer sun ripens clusters of grapes, the fruit falls (or is picked), and the yearly cycle begins again."

The students were able to draw parallels between winter and their own desire to hide away at home with a book or—more likely—Nintendo, and between spring and their own height increases, hair growth, and emotional development, and between summer and their own desire to rest and hang out doing nothing in the restful hours of intense sun-filled days.

"How do you think the mountain wilderness and forests function without the involvement of man?" I asked them. They concluded that the four seasons and their cycles provided all that was needed to maintain the complex balance of nature: nutritious soil and healthy plant and animal life.

"Most of the time," I said. I explained to them how I'd learned that administering manmade chemical products did not work for my vineyard, but neither did doing nothing; instead, I'd found a workable yearly guide that fulfilled my desires to let the seasons progress naturally and encourage their natural processes, and actually made my grapevines healthier. This entailed composting and cover cropping in the late fall (with plants that would later supply the nutrients they needed), pruning in the winter using a style that encouraged their strength given my specific terrain, mowing down the cover crop, turning the soil around the base of the vines, weed burning (with a creative propane burner that turns the weeds into ash), shoot thinning vines that achieved overly vigorous spring growth, and irrigating only when absolutely necessary.

"I believe that because of the particular farming choices I've made, my grape flavors have changed," I told the students. My particular farming techniques are embodied in the art of the finished wine and this invisible characteristic makes my grapes, and the wine produced from my grapes, completely unique." I went on to tell the kids that I can present this dogma to any outsider, stomp my feet and shake my head, however, it will probably make no sense unless I actually tell them what went into the transformation of those grapes, the years of turmoil I experienced, and the decades of growth that I instilled upon my fruit. The fruit from my Merlot grapes has changed over the years. They no longer have the same immature taste; instead, they are complicated, adventurous, and vehement—just like me. "But like the changing tides, that could all be different next year," I said, "and this, I think, is the mystique that surrounds grape-growing and the entire wine world."

The students sent me thank you notes with comments ranging from "I didn't know that the natural cycles of the seasons could help the soil," to "It's very interesting to incorporate the seasons in growing things," to "I never thought the seasons were very important until you told us about what they do." And without knowing how much it would touch me, one student wrote, "I thought the talk was great, but I really loved your outfit."

FOURTEEN

THE GRAPE IS ALWAYS RIPER IN THE OTHER VINEYARD

*L*ife is like Mother Nature—I recently reminded myself quietly— filled with valleys, plains, and storms. And because of this I think it seems as though everyone else has the perfect existence and they have all the answers to life's capricious problems. I want to be in someone else's body because from the outside looking in everyone else seems so happy; I can't see or feel their confusion or pain. This is an illusion—I know. I tell myself that I can cope because certain truths are not to be accepted; they are to be challenged and fought with. And this is progress. I fight with my own reasoning each moment.

My kids say that my grapes and wine are "hella" good. As we were all sweeping out the garage, stacking heaps of junk into keep and throw away piles, I asked my Grace and Dude, "Is 'hella' a word?"

"Of course, it's part of our language," they say.

"You have your own language now?" I question. I already know this is not so far-fetched because I have my own language, too. It's prose that only I know at this very moment; a biting tongue that barks things like, "If I were compost, I'd poison the soil," and "If I were water, I'd kill the plants," and "If I were wine, I'd turn men into swine."

I was spellbound by my own thoughts, wearily allowing myself to drift off into a bit of a dazed state. Three weeks earlier I had come down with a pain that had overtaken the left side of my body and resulted in a mostly bedridden state as I awaited various treatments and allowed myself to rest. This was the first day I was attempting to do a little cleaning, though the kids were doing most of the work.

I was startled out of my thought process when I saw Grace suddenly standing in front of me with a shovel in her hand. "I'm going to chop its head off, Mom," she shouted.

I had been completely oblivious to the fact that as we were standing there, a lethal—seemingly fearless—scaly creature had crawled out of the folds of an old dusty tent. My lack of response led me to wonder if my body's numbness was seeping into my emotions, too. Like a deer frozen by the blinding headlights of an oncoming car, I was unable to budge. Everything moved in slow motion as I felt a longing to travel backwards in time and find the place in my life where I had been the happiest—a point when I was free from pain, free from the fear of death, and free from the stymie of not knowing anything about my present destiny.

I was fascinated by the juxtaposition that I was facing at that precise moment, that of my life and my existence both being in danger, and my numbness to it being utterly overwhelming.

"Are you sure, I mean are we absolutely certain," I heard myself saying more slowly than normal, "that this snake is actually a rattler?

Because I don't want to kill it unless it's a dangerous threat." My thoughts sluggishly turned to the king snake I'd slaughtered, and my greatest convictions about preserving nature.

"Yes, Mom," Dude said. "Look at the diamond-shaped head—and the rattler."

Rattlesnakes are venomous snakes with diamond-shaped heads and segmented tails that rattle when vibrated—or when they're disrupted and ready to attack. As we discussed it, the rattler moved closer. I couldn't speak or move. It was tightly coiled with its head inches from my body, ready to take a bite out of my calf, only barely covered by my bathrobe. The rattle was shaking and the tip of the tail was moving rapidly back and forth. My lack of emotion was cause for concern from all my children. "Mom," Dude said, "let it out; tell us what you're thinking. We need to know what you want us to do."

"Shasta! Fudge! Doggonnit!" I screamed. "This is not right, this is not fair, this is abuse!" Was I talking about my physical situation or the coiled reptile? All that mattered was that it felt good to scream. "Kill the dang snake!" I yelled. "Let's take control of this thing and make it go away." In my mind I was yelling for everything to go away, for the pain to stop, for my life back, but the cue was all the kids needed to go in for the attack.

Grace and Dude took turns pounding the rattlesnake with our small, garden shovel while Joy clicked photos of the scene. My children took care of me; they were protectors, take-charge proprietors of the dwelling, and forthright captains of the ship. I was wearing my sheer bathrobe in only bare feet because the weather was warm, and because that had been my outfit of choice for the last few weeks of my life. Since I'd been relegated to my bed by the numbness and tingling all over the

243

left side of my body, and by neck pain that had turned me into an invalid, I hadn't been in street clothes—or farm clothes—for nearly four weeks. Bedridden meant (to me) that I was allowed to wander around my home, cluttered garage included, when no one was looking. And this made me notice, regrettably, that my confined quarters needed organization—for aesthetic purposes and for purposes of cleansing the fragile state of my emotional turmoil. It became clear that the space I lived in needed to provide me with a soothing haven and an uncomplicated environment where I could heal.

Once the deed was done, we had new troubles. Our car was filled with rubbish—loaded up and bound for the junk pile at the dump— and more than likely there were additional baby snakes tucked away in various folds and crevices of the rancid-smelling drop clothes and plastic coverings that had already been loaded into the backseat of our truck before we spied the rattler. This was an alarming thought, and one that actually made me think of abandoning my vehicle in an oak meadow someplace on my property. "We could think of it as art deco and use it as a funky support system for climbing roses or we could let some of the wild animals on our property use it as a refuge away from the winter rains and blustery weather," I said aloud. It was a nice thought. We left the snake there and gained enough courage to drive the car to the dump, luckily without any unforeseen incidents.

✳ ✳ ✳

"You must keep your life placid and free of all stress, Mrs. Moulton," the doctor said, before he stuck the needle somewhere in the spinal area of my neck to inject medicine that would help my disk inflammation. I'd already been told to slow down my pace or else I risked permanent numbness and possible paralysis. The "what ifs" were too much. It was three days after the snake episode and I could still picture the snake lying on my garage floor. "Sure thing," I heard myself say, disbelieving, "I have a very low-key, tranquil life." This was untrue. The doctors had finally located my problem and I could certainly deal with the fact that I had a collapsed disk in my neck that had taken a chunk out of my spinal cord, pinched a bunch of nerves, and made me reevaluate my own mortality. I tried to convince myself that I could sculpt my life around a peaceful environment. How could I alleviate the daily excitement of farm life? I could hire a farmhand to help me with the daily chores, or I could leave the work undone until I was better, or I could pay my children to help me with my daily routines. There were solutions, I said to myself, and all I need is time, and rest, and a few simple lifestyle changes. I wanted to believe that I could change my malfunctioning neck into a perfectly functioning body part without letting the doctor's cut into my spine and graft a piece of my pelvis onto my vertebrae.

"My life has become too complicated," I told Chuck one night when I couldn't move my left arm anymore and couldn't sleep because the pain was so intense. As of this summer, 2003, we have sixty acres of land—twenty-four acres in Glen Ellen and thirty-six in the Carneros region of Sonoma. The thirty-six acres we'd bought two years before when I'd hoped to plant more grapes and progress to bigger scale farming was land we harvested hay on for a nearby dairy. That land, straddling two California winegrowing regions— Napa and Sonoma—with its fertile, virgin soils, was considered to be one of California's most famous grape-growing regions. Filled

with history and situated across the road from Sangiacomo's vineyards, one of the leading grape-growers in the region with over a
thousand acres of grapes, the land is ideal for cool to moderate
growing varieties like Sauvignon Blanc, Chardonnay, and Pinot
Noir. But the fluctuations in the economy, the war, and the uncer-
tainty of grape prices, had forced us to slow down the project. Three
wells, two septic systems, our home in Glen Ellen, and structures in
Carneros, including a one hundred-year-old farmhouse (I'd
restored), a two-story tankhouse (I was restoring), and a 6,500-
square-foot decrepit dairy, have kept me overly busy recently.

"Let's move to the farmhouse, sell Glen Ellen, and pursue our
goal of planting more grapes," I blurted out. The old farmhouse surrounded by thriving vineyards and feminine hillsides had changed
from a badly neglected structure situated on what was once the
stagecoach trail from San Francisco to Sonoma to a bright and
cheery yellow home with white picket fencing, arbors, and hundreds
of sparkling grapevines. It had been a big project, but one that had
earned the structure historical restorations awards and the pride that
a one hundred-year-old farmhouse in the Sonoma wine country
should have.

"I don't know," Chuck said hesitantly. This is the guy who hates
change so much that he won't even buy new shoes unless the holes
on the bottom get so big that his feet start getting abrasions from
the ground. "It seems a bit crazy, but if it would simplify your
life...." He was still gone at work nearly ninety hours a week.

"I'll take what I've learned and move on—otherwise my life
could become mundane and boring," I responded, trying to pad my
present situation, look to the future, and remain optimistic. "My

reality has become the sum of all the things I have learned about this piece of land, and all that I have no power to change." I recognize that change really has become my matter; challenge has become my place.

"I think you might be right," he acquiesced, willing to say anything just to make me feel better. We sampled a friendly Merlot from Leveroni Vineyards and a vibrant Syrah from Little Vineyards hoping to find inspiration in these new wines whose families have been in the farming business for three and four generations, but they have just decided to, along with selling their grapes, take a stab at producing and selling their own wine. They offer us the hope that we, or our children, may some day make wine to sell from our grapes and continue on in the business as they have.

"This house and piece of land are nothing if we can't all continue to learn new things and broaden our scope through change," I said. I realize that this is what has made our family grow together. "And besides, I'm rushing too much; I'm not really seeing things and the darn lavender isn't able to calm me down anymore."

I feel like I will need to take the fruit from past harvests and the memories of the past ten years with me, pack them away in a suitcase, and have them with me later to bathe in their juices like some weary traveler desperate for a cleansing. A good friend of mine once told me she felt this way when she left her home, and to soothe her aching heart she dug up ten or so grapevines and moved them along with her other personal items. My grapevines have become a personal item.

* * *

Rachel recently called and offered to come and take care of me. She has already given so much to my family—her time, her love, and her wisdom.

"Nope," I tell her, "I'm taking the knowledge that I've gained from being the caretaker of this land, and I'm gonna spread it around, and share it with other pieces of land."

"I understand," she says. "Don't you feel a remarkable peace in knowing that you've figured out another way to learn, and grow, and continue farming?"

"Yes, I have definitely outgrown this land." It's comforting to say this out loud. Rachel already knows that what I really mean is that I've outgrown this period of my life—not the land. But I will farm my new land, once my neck has healed and my mobility is back, and I will do it my way from start to finish. She can hear the excitement in my voice when I tell her that on my next property I intend to plant grapes on virgin land—where the cows have roamed for hundreds of years—seriously contemplate my options, and maybe even farm biodynamically.

"I might even plant Rhone-style varieties and make my own wine—reminiscent of Southern France," I say smiling to myself. There's nothing like really seeing something for the first time. "Chuck will fight me, Rachel, he'll want to plant mainstream grapes, but I'll win. I always do."

✳ ✳ ✳

Days after the epidural procedure in my neck there is no more talk about moving and I seem to be getting better. We finally managed to toss the snake over our three-foot rock wall into the tall grass that lay behind it. The turkey vultures must have found it and consumed it right away, since it was gone the next day. The buzzards consume every decaying corpse left on my property, and I've learned to appreciate their unsolicited garbage service. Unlike the gobbling ground turkeys, these dark plumed, large birds fly overhead—with their six-foot wingspan—darting in and out of our rolling hills and thick brush. Many mornings I see two or three of them perched on my large wooden vineyard posts at the end of my grapevine rows. Their bare, red heads twisting around scanning the vineyard for untouched carcasses of mice, rats, squirrels, and you name it, left from the night. I've seen groups of them consume a dead deer in minutes, leaving just the bones to decompose and dissolve into the soil.

Because of the remarkable efficiency of these birds, I've never worried about the rotting cadavers of animals polluting my vineyard. The real concern for grapevines comes from transient disease spread by living pathogenic organisms like fungi, viruses, and bacteria. Vines are a host for these pathogens, and the susceptibility of individual grapevines depends upon grape variety and the region where the grapes are grown. The diseases these pathogens produce can induce grapevine nutrient imbalance and environmental stress that eventually causes unhealthy vines, bad fruit, and sometimes death. Fungi are transmitted to vines through direct contact of tissue or wound and natural openings, and they survive off of living parts of the vine or dead parts left on the ground. Inserted through grapevine wounds or bad propagation, viruses are transmitted by insect vectors that leave particles of the disease on the vine that eventually multiply by using resources from their host. Bacteria is transmitted by insects or water, entering through wounds or openings on the vine. And just like dealing with many human ailments, there are ways to identify and cope with certain grapevine diseases. By maintaining healthy plants, lowering the stress of the vines, and using simple vineyard management practices, one can gain control over unwanted, life-threatening grapevine diseases with simple organic processes.

FUNGI, VIRUSES, AND BACTERIA

Diseases Caused from Fungi

NOBLE ROT OR GRAY-MOLD ROT (*BOTRYTIS CINEREA*)

Found in vineyards all over the world, this fungus likes temperatures of 69–80 degrees Fahrenheit and 70–80% humidity, and generally occurs during wet springs, bloomtime, or harvest (if it rains).

SIGNS TO WATCH FOR

Buds and shoots become dried out and brown in the spring. Leaves turn brown, shoots sometimes begin to die, and clusters drop off the vine. The berry shrinks and becomes very concentrated with sugars and acids. The disease generally lowers quality and quantity of crop, but has also been known to produce exceptional wines like the Sauternes in France.

HOW THE DISEASE IS TRANSFERRED

At bloomtime, the spores float through the air and land on the flowers. Spores enter via the ovary. Other ways of transmission are by puncture wounds to the berries during *veraison* (see page 134) and onward, or by the orange tortrix moth, which feeds on the berries and causes a point of entry for the fungus.

TECHNIQUES FOR PREVENTION

Leaf pluck to keep leaves away from ripening clusters and to allow more aeration and sun exposure to the berries. Maintain a good open canopy trellis system that encourages aeration and sun exposure. Leaf plucking and good open trellis systems encourage the skin on the berries to thicken and makes it more difficult for the spores to penetrate.

OAK-ROOT FUNGUS
(*ARMILLARIA MELLEA*)

Although this fungus is thought to be native to California, it is found in temperate climates around the world.

SIGNS TO WATCH FOR

Never grows on top of bark, always under bark. Lives in xylem, cambium, and phloem and can be seen if you peel back the bark. There will be white, fan-looking marks and a mushroom-like odor once the bark is peeled back. The bacteria wipes out the transport system of the vine and it can eventually girdle and kill the plant.

HOW THE DISEASE IS TRANSFERRED

The fungus survives on the roots and woody parts of oak trees, walnut trees, and pine trees. It can also be transmitted from movement of roots by equipment or moving water.

TECHNIQUES FOR PREVENTION

Don't plant vines around oak, walnut, or pine trees. If these trees are present around vines and vines start to die, cut into the bark for positive determination. Remove sick vine, as well as the two vines next to it, and replant.

DOWNY MILDEW
(*PLASMOPARA VITICOLA*)

Native to eastern North America, but is found in most grape-growing regions in the world—except California.

SIGNS TO WATCH FOR

Fungus attacks petioles, shoots, leaves, and berries. The leaves look wet and have white fuzz on their underside. The tissue on the leaves dies and the leaves turn brown and drop to the ground. Because the fruit is unable to ripen without leaves, the crop is seriously affected.

HOW THE DISEASE IS TRANSFERRED

Spores need a wet environment to germinate and are transferred from the soil after rain. They multiply rapidly in prolonged wet weather.

TECHNIQUES FOR PREVENTION

Remove dead leaves around vines and keep vines dry during

rain in spring and summer by exposing them to sunlight or aeration. Maintain good ground sanitation by removing leaves and old berries in late fall, and by cultivating ground (removing debris) in early spring.

EUTYPA DIEBACK OR DEAD-ARM (*PHOMOPSIS VITICOLA*)

Found in regions of the world where winters are harsh, and also in more moderate climates.

SIGNS TO WATCH FOR

Appears soon after budburst. Leaves become chlorotic with brown spots, and are tattered-looking and misshapen. The shoots are stunted with short internodes. Berries don't ripen and wood on the vine dies.

HOW THE DISEASE IS TRANSFERRED

Spores can travel up to 100 miles. They get into vine after pruning in the winter (when there is rain, dampness, or dew).

TECHNIQUES FOR PREVENTION

Avoid pruning when there is rain. In cooler regions, try to prune as early as possible, and don't make large pruning cuts. If you see the fungus on the vine, then prune below the infected area and make sure to burn all prunings.

BLACK ROT
(GUIGNARDIA BIDWELLII)

Found in eastern United States or regions of the world with moist, rainy summer weather.

SIGNS TO WATCH FOR

Causes reddish-brown spots on the leaves or ulcer-like cankers on the shoots and cluster stems. Berries dry up, shrivel, and become hard and sunken.

HOW THE DISEASE IS TRANSFERRED

Fungus grows best in hot, moist summer weather or places where summer rain can carry the spores.

TECHNIQUES FOR PREVENTION

Burn prunings and turn soil in early spring (buries disease-producing fungus).

POWDERY MILDEW
(UNCINULA NECATOR)

Found in dry climates of the world, this mildew is a nuisance for California grape-growers.

SIGNS TO WATCH FOR

This fungus likes warm days and cool nights, and lives at

45–92 degrees Fahrenheit with anywhere from 0–99% humidity. It causes a white, fuzzy fungus on the upper side of leaf, and produces yellow, black, and brown spots on the leaves, and scarring marks on the underside of leaves.

HOW THE DISEASE IS TRANSFERRED

Spores travel in the air and are transported by wind. They attach to leaves, shoots, and berries on the vine.

TECHNIQUES FOR PREVENTION

This fungus develops rapidly in shade. Long exposure to the sun will kill it (temperatures over 100 degrees Fahrenheit). Organic farmers as well as traditional farmers sulfur dust to control this fast-growing fungus. Some farmers dust at less then 6 inches of shoot growth and every 7–10 days thereafter until no later than 6 weeks pre-harvest (if any closer to harvest it can cause wine that smells like stinky socks and tastes like rotten eggs). Others dust at 6, 12, 18, and 24 inches of shoot growth and 14 days thereafter until 6 weeks pre-harvest. Commercial farmers use 5–10 pounds of sulfur per acre, but small growers need only to put a fine dust on the their leaves, shoots, and clusters of the vine. Keeping the area around the vines free from old berries, dead wood, and dead leaves helps remove spores.

> * Never dust if the temperatures are 95 degrees Farenheit or over, and if it rains afer dusting, redo the dusting once the weather stops and the air dries.

Diseases Caused from Viruses

FANLEAF VIRUS: SPREAD IN SOIL AND FOUND ALL OVER THE WORLD

SIGNS TO WATCH FOR

Creates widening of petiole sinus with serrations around the edge of leaves (leaf looks like an open fan), and zigzag shoots with short internodes and splits in the shoots. Leaves can also develop what is called a yellow mosaic, which is bright chrome yellow discolorations of the leaves, shoots, and tendrils. Vine becomes large, but there is very little crop (all energy goes into wood production).

HOW THE DISEASE IS TRANSFERRED

Transmitted by the Xiphinema index nematode and from infected wood used for propagation.

TECHNIQUES FOR PREVENTION

Buy virus-free grapevines.

LEAFROLL VIRUS

Airborne and found all over the world.

SIGNS TO WATCH FOR

Plants are smaller than normal. The disease causes chronic

loss of crop. In the late spring, the leaves roll downward and they are red, yellow, and chloratic.

HOW THE DISEASE IS TRANSFERRED

Transmitted through propagation and is not spread from one vine to another, but the vine must be infected at the time of propagation.

TECHNIQUES FOR PREVENTION

Buy stock from registered mother vines that are free of the virus.

CORKY BARK

Transmitted through grafting.

SIGNS TO WATCH FOR

Symptoms on leaves are same as leafroll: red, yellow, and chloratic. Death occurs at graft union where bark, once peeled back, is swollen, puffy, cork-like, and pitted.

HOW THE DISEASE IS TRANSFERRED

Transmitted through propagation and is not spread from one vine to another.

TECHNIQUES FOR PREVENTION

Buy stock from registered mother vines that are free of the virus.

Diseases Caused from Bacteria

CROWN GALL

Found in temperate winegrowing places where freeze injury occurs.

SIGNS TO WATCH FOR

Galls appear on the crown of the vine, or various places on the trunk or arms. The gall tissue is spongy, lumpy, soft, and disorganized. Often it appears light colored and then turns dark, and is much like a cancerous growth.

HOW THE DISEASE IS TRANSFERRED

Pruning cuts allow entry of the bacteria. Frost and moist weather can also cause wood to split, which provides another point of entry.

TECHNIQUES FOR PREVENTION

Keep pruning equipment clean by using a chlorine solution. Disinfect tools by dipping into solution between pruning each vine. If galls are present, do not cut into them during pruning (can spread disease). Most galls disappear after a couple of years.

PIERCE'S DISEASE
(BLUE-GREEN SHARPSHOOTER VECTOR)

This disease is also known as Anaheim's disease since it was first found in Anaheim, California, in the late 1800s. It has been found mostly in the Americas.

SIGNS TO WATCH FOR

Bud break is delayed by two weeks. Leaves turn yellow and brown, and fall off leaving the petioles still attached to the shoot. This bacteria plugs the xylem and the tissue dries out from lack of water. Leaves are scalded causing poor vigor, less crop, and eventually death. The disease causes irregular, patchy bark maturation, and green patches at the node area. In the fall, the leaves turn red because the areas that move water to the leaves become blocked.

HOW THE DISEASE IS TRANSFERRED

Outbreaks are usually worse after wet springs. Bacteria is carried by the blue-green sharpshooters, a type of leaf hopper. These insects can be found in riparian habitats and they get their bacteria, called Xylella fastidiosa, from periwinkle, willow trees, and blackberries. Generally doesn't travel more than 150 feet.

TECHNIQUES FOR PREVENTION

Replant with resistant grapes. Control the vector with yellow, sticky traps placed along creek beds, rivers, or stream areas, and monitor once a week. Provide vegetation alternatives so that insects won't be attracted to grapevines.

PIERCE'S DISEASE
(GLASSY-WINGED SHARPSHOOTER VECTOR)

Found mostly in California regions.

SIGNS TO WATCH FOR

Same as those caused by bacteria introduced by blue-green sharpshooter vector.

HOW THE DISEASE IS TRANSFERRED

Same as that of blue-green sharpshooter, but the glassy-winged sharpshooter—a half-inch long leaf hopper—can travel greater distances and consume larger amounts of plant sap per day.

TECHNIQUES FOR PREVENTION

As of yet, there are no resistant grapevines. This vector is an extreme worry for grape-growers living in California. Grapevines die quickly from starvation and dehydration. Farmers are using yellow, sticky traps and nurseries are being closely monitored for the dangerous leaf hoppers. There is a plan to bring in an insect called the fairy wasp, which reportedly destroys the sharpshooter eggs.

There seems to be a common theme of how to treat fungi, viruses, and bacteria that are a threat to wine grapevines. Keep the vines healthy by providing good sun exposure, proper aeration, healthy soil with lots of living organisms, and sanitary ground environments (remove old debris). And also, buy virus-free grapevines from registered nurseries.

FIFTEEN

MAY THE HARVEST BE WITH YOU

*H*arvest, besides conjuring up thoughts of stomping grapes, soaking in all the pungent smells of the valley, and basking in the warmth of the sun, means hard work. Once it's been determined that it's time to pick, anywhere from late August to late November in Sonoma wine country, the crews line up at various places around the valley. A picker's pay is directly related to the quantity of grapes they bring in, and it takes skill to work quickly and not bruise the fruit. The workers drop their plastic bins under the vine, and with a sharp, half-mooned tool they slash away at the stems while the heavy fruit drops into their container. When they fill a plastic bin, they hoist the heavy container onto the top of their head, and run to their field manager exchanging fruit for a claim ticket that they quickly stuff under their hat. The tickets collected at the end of the day will be exchanged for money. Most of the fieldworkers are immigrants from Mexico who are trained in agricultural work back in their native country. They work from dawn to dusk, or they work all night and sleep during the day. Grape-pickers work hard. Hard work clears the mind. Grape-pickers must have clear heads and strength of mind to do their job well.

The fruit is hurried to the winery like rushing late travelers on their way to catch an early train. There's no time to waste, every minute counts, the longer the grapes are in transit the more flavor they will lose and the more rot will occur. In the Sonoma region, car drivers halt for trucks loaded with fruit, "Let them go first," we tell our young children, in preparation for when they learn to drive in the valley, "they are carrying the fruits of our land and we are just the spectators—we'll have to wait."

"An overturned grape truck on highway 116," the radio blares, while the listeners cringe fearing it may be one of theirs filled with thousands of dollars worth of fruit. Growers stop on the highway as they pass one another in their pick-up trucks, "How's your crop? Does the fruit taste good? Not too much mold this year? Let's celebrate— soon," they shout at each other, while traffic stops behind them.

There's no time to cook and barely time to eat, so the "La Bamba" and "Jesus" burrito trucks follow the farm workers with their portable restaurant composed of an enclosed truck filled with a full kitchen packed with fresh avocados, tomatoes, spicy red salsa, rice, beans, and various meats. We follow the trucks into other peoples' vineyards for our own dinner of carne asada tacos, chili verde and black beans, fresh corn tortillas with melted cheese and fresh salsa, and Mexican sodas. Everyone stands around eating and craning their necks to watch the hot air balloons float by while the sweaty crews of pickers descend on the trucks, steam spewing from

WHAT HAPPENS TO GRAPES BEFORE HARVEST?

Grape Berry Development Is Divided Into Stages

GREEN STAGE

This period lasts anywhere from 5–7 weeks. The berries are green and hard; they enlarge rapidly; and the sugars are low and the acids are high.

VERAISON

French for berry color change, veraison lasts 2–4 weeks. The berries soften and start changing color. The sugar levels increase and acid levels remain high.

RIPE STAGE

This period is marked by the final growth in berry size and lasts anywhere from 5–8 weeks. The berries become softer, sugars continue to rise, acidity levels drop, the skin in red varieties becomes red, and the aroma of the berry is attained.

OVERRIPE STAGE

Acidity levels continue to drop; sugars remain stable. The berry begins to shrivel.

What Factors Influence Ripening Grapes?

- Cold weather delays maturation dates—regardless of variety
- Overwatering delays ripening
- Heavier crop load delays maturation
- Underwatering speeds up ripening
- Training techniques that allow more sunlight exposure speeds up ripening
- Nitrogen deficiency speeds up maturation

WHEN DO I HARVEST?

Some small-scale winemakers make wine without testing any grape levels; instead, they pick the fruit based on sweetness, texture, and aroma, and whether the calendar shows that harvest time has arrived. But here are some technical indications that professionals might use.

SUGAR LEVELS

Grapes should be picked when sugars reach the optimal level for winemaking. The sugars that are fermentable in the grapes consist of glucose (dextrose) and fructose (levulose). Some people say to start testing the percentage sugar of the grapes, also called Balling or Brix, after veraison and on a weekly basis thereafter. Optimal sugar levels for white wines are around 21–24 Brix, and for red wines they are around 23–26 Brix.

* Anything over 28 Brix can cause spoilage problems if fermentation shuts down before fermentable sugars have been converted to alcohol. On the other hand, grape juices that do not have enough percentage sugar (18 Brix or less) can produce wines that are simplistic, poor tasting, and unstable.

ACID LEVELS

Malic acid and tartaric acid, along with traces of other acids, are the two major acids that provide the tartness found in many wines. The total acids (TA) help to protect the wine from organisms that can cause spoilage of the wine. The figures for total acidity should range from 0.5–0.8%. Fruit that is under-ripe tends to be more acidic, and fruit that is over-ripe tends to be less acidic.

pH LEVELS

An acceptable range for pH is from 3.1–3.6. The pH is considered the measurement for the wines' stability and resistance to bacterial spoilage. Grapes that have very low pH values may have problems with fermentation, and those with high pH values will be more likely to have problems with spoilage.

the open window as the single chef produces fresh food faster than a fast food restaurant.

* * *

I remember interviewing a picker—long before I had my own grapes—for a school project. Now that I've picked myself, I know what backbreaking work it really is. But at that time, I didn't truly understand what it was about. The fellow's name I interviewed was Jesus, and although he told me how pickers require endurance and lots of strength, he also shared with me his feelings about why someone would choose a job that is so rigorous and difficult.

"It's tradition," he told me, "it's memories that become timeless, like when you open a bottle of wine today and remember back twenty years ago toasting with a friend who is now gone, and it's pride in being involved with something that is intricately woven with one's heritage, religion, and history." Jesus explained, "You know, some farm workers leave their families behind for nine months at a time, and some take their families with them because they can't bear to be without them for so long, but no matter which they choose, their hearts are in it for these reasons." His motives, those from a culture completely different than mine, are the exact same reasons why I became involved with grape-growing and winemaking. And I realize that this business bonds people from different places of the world; we share a commonality like no other trade I know of.

Jesus made me realize that most of us involved with grape-growing and winemaking are in it because we feel a duty and a sense of passion for continuing the customs of our ancestors: their food

BEFORE HARVEST, HOW DO I CHECK THE SUGAR, ACID, AND pH LEVELS OF MY GRAPES?

To Test Sugars

One can use a refractometer or hydrometer purchased from winemaking stores.

HYDROMETER

The best type of hydrometer to purchase is the triple-scale hydrometer that has three different readings: specific gravity, percent sugar by weight (also called Balling or Brix), and potential alcohol by volume. This instrument measures the Balling or Brix of the juice and gives sugar contents of the berry liquid (also can be used for determining the alcohol content of the wine by subtracting the alcohol reading before fermentation and after fermentation). Growers pick berries from the middle of bunches from different vines in their vineyard (in order to represent variations of sunlight exposure, and the cooler and warmer mesoclimates within the vineyard). Four ounces of juice are needed to get a reading and the berries must be crushed and put through a sieve before putting into the glass or plastic test jar of hydrometer kit. Place the hydrometer into the test jar and swirl it around before taking a reading—making sure there are no carbon dioxide bubbles present that could cause the hydrometer to pop up higher in the liquid. As the hydrometer settles, take the reading at the liquid level from the top of the test jar. Take a reading for sugar and potential alcohol. Since the hydrometer is calibrated at 60 degrees Fahrenheit, and you might not know the temperature of your berry juice, use the conversion chart for temperature variations that comes with the kit.

REFRACTOMETER

A hand refractometer measures soluble sugars by using refracted light as it passes through the juice. It is more costly than the hydrometer, but requires less work to read the sugar levels of the juice. (Before using the refractometer, standardize the settings by using a couple of drops of distilled water. While in direct sunlight, look through the eyepiece and make sure the sugar scale reads zero (adjust the screws until it does).

To Test Acids

The winemakers' supply stores carry acid test kits, which is all you need to test the acids.

To Test pH

Purchase pH strips at a wine supply store. Find strips with the narrowest range.

and drink rituals, their religious ceremonies, and their spirited pro-
tocols for family gatherings. And because we want to celebrate with
each other over the fruits of our labor; we want to talk about how
we overcame the hardships of Mother Nature and were able to produce a healthy crop and a great bottle of wine; we want to take a
brief moment in our lives to respect our compelling flavors and
share them with one another; and most of all, we want to rejoice
over the benevolence of our land.

This is why, to this day, after all these years of being in this business, I still go nuts when I lose fruit just before harvest.

"The stork is in the vineyard, and it's eating the grapes!" Dude yelled.
This was last year at harvest time. It came from a joke we'd harbored
many years ago when my kids referred to all birds on our property
as "storks." They thought these birds to be exotic in appearance and
the delivery service for babies. I decided, after Joy had entered nursery school, that the two older kids, and Joy too, should not continue
thinking that storks brought babies. They thought my discussion of
the birds and the bees so far-fetched that they hounded me for years
with the stork brings baby story—insisting that it was the way it was
done. Hence, the stork has become our code word for any out-of-
the-ordinary birds on our property—and a subtle reference to
important issues concerning sex.

"Stork?" I asked sarcastically. "Oh really, Dude?" wondering if
he had a question about sex. It isn't often that Dude shares his
thoughts and feelings about sex with me these days, and sure

enough, he was talking about strange-looking birds in the vineyard—wild turkeys. "Shasta!" I yelled. "They're back!"

I cringe at the thought of how many grapes I never get to pluck off the vine because of those wild turkeys. I anguish about the fruit smells I never get to revel in, their fragrant juices exploding into the air. Try as I do, I just can't forget—even for the sake of a starving turkey—how I've endured and labored for that one special moment when I will have that fruit in my sweaty, anxious palm. That a wild turkey insists on taking it away from me is much too frustrating. And I've often asked myself these questions: Can I beat these animals at their own game? Can I make them see things my way? Should I harass them until they fly onto someone else's property? There are no easy answers.

Several years ago I became so angry at harvest time that I started putting up orange traffic cones wherever I found turkey droppings in an attempt to provide proof that they were a significant detriment to my livelihood and vineyard. In order to legally remove certain animal pests, farmers must obtain a valid permit from a specific county agency. The cones were a desperate attempt to gain the attention of the Fish and Game people. Their acknowledgment would grant me permission to remove the devious animals that insisted on munching my fruit every summer.

"We hit one of your traffic cones—again," my parents sighed as they walked in the house, invited over for a summertime dinner. It put me in a bad mood right away.

"Can't you just go around the cones like everyone else?" I asked edgily. They'd already encouraged me to remove the markers for the convenience of guests. "During harvest, Mom, I care about my grapes!" I declared. They didn't understand how I could prioritize my grapes over my guests' convenience.

This also means that for harvest (in my ten years of experience, anyway) neither man nor any of his inventions are necessary for determining grape sugar levels. We have an unconventional sugar-testing program—without the gadgetry. Wild turkeys, joined by deer, both feel obliged to sample and make their own evaluations about whether the fruit is savory and mellow, or whether it needs more time to hang on the vine. I always know the response of the animals based on if they return the next day to the same area, or if they move on to sample a new spot. And I've found that these animals have an uncanny aptitude for judging grapes; unfortunately, they are the same grapes that I want, and the ones that would make the most flavorful wine—perfect sugar levels, perfect acid levels, and perfect pH levels.

But as time has gone on, I recognize that what I once thought was a tragic scenario, when it came to animals feasting on my grapes, was really a blessing. My means of persuasion came from a reality that was genuine and consummate, and one that arrived when I was least expecting it. Just minutes away from our home is a land retreat called Bouverie Preserve, a picture-perfect setting that was donated by a man named Bouverie as a place for school children to go and learn about nature and the merits of wildlife. There are hundreds of acres filled with spiritual Native American waterfalls and trails leading from one paradise to another. Joy and I had the privilege of hiking its trails with her fourth grade class. As our tour guide was leading us through areas covered with oak tree meadows that slowly transformed into redwood forests, she chatted on about the magnificent animals that paraded through that special piece of land. "There are mountain lions, bobcats, deer, coyotes, jack rabbits, fox, woodpeckers, hawks, turkeys, and bats," she said.

"Mom," Joy said, turning around to grab my arm, "we have *all* those animals on our farm!"

One of her classmates, overhearing her asked skeptically, "You mean you've actually seen a bobcat on your property?"

"Not only on our property, but standing at our back door," I said. Joy suddenly became the center of attention when everyone heard this.

"They're incredibly cool," she said. "They have a spotted reddish-brown coat, and white, silky paws with black stripes between their claws."

Tourists come from all over to climb the trails of Bouverie Preserve in hot pursuit of catching a glimpse of the exotic wildlife. Most of them go away having only seen traces of animal scat. And me, I've fought for years to keep these wild animals away just to preserve the fruit from my grapevines. I never realized that the rest of the world would covet the chance to see even one of these animals—if only for a brief moment. I'd been living with them for so long, it never occurred to me that I was blessed with their presence—not cursed. This was definitely a convincing thought that I had for so long viewed as otherwise.

I do finally see the merits of my own pasture now—even if I have to share some of my fruit at harvest time.

SIXTEEN

I CAME, I SAW, I DRANK

*W*hen I first came to the Sonoma wine country and started growing grapes, I learned that crush is every grape-grower's friend; it's a moment in time when the grape is finally transformed and brought to life through its expression in wine. The farmer gets to speculate on the romance that will follow if the game is played correctly. The grape goes through a metamorphosis that transfigures it into a more glamorous state. This shift from grape-growing to winemaking can be compared to the expectant anguish that ultimately arrives after putting the icing on the cake (that nearly sunk) and putting the whipped cream atop the milkshake (that almost melted) and squirting the catsup on the meatloaf (that nearly burned). For me, besides relishing the feelings that this time brings, it means that I will no longer need to continue chasing vermin around the yard, picking helpless bugs off the vine, hunting them down in the wee hours of the night, counting ants using a magnifying glass, or spending my days chatting these crazy weeds through the harsh seasons. Now I'll think about whether I want to wear shoes during crush, and whether I want to stomp my grapes while I dance under the light of the moon. Or would I rather feast on wild edibles with my mother and sip old vintages with my father, while my children take over the job of releasing the juices from the grapes?

The first year I made wine I received a bronze medal at the Sonoma County Harvest Wine Fair. It was an extreme surprise, and I can honestly say that although I tried to follow many of the winemaking skills I had learned in viticulture school, I still made many mistakes. One of my favorite analogies to the success of winemaking has to do with this simple concept. Take three children from the same family and ask them how they view their mother. The answer will fall anywhere from "she was the greatest" to "she raised us in a very dysfunctional manner." Yet, each of the children will have an entirely believable and rational story. How could this be—three people with entirely different perceptions of the same person? In terms of winemaking, take three winemakers with the same grapes and the wine will be completely different. Because it represents their personalities and is a statement of each of their voices, as well as a creative outlet for their artistic desires, there will be few similarities. And the drinkers of those wines will have entirely different perspectives concerning the taste and excellence of the flavor. People who make wine have their own ways of getting to the end result, and no matter what guidelines one has previously been given, it's hard to follow the strokes of someone else's paintbrush.

I was always told by other winemakers that before progressing after harvest it's imperative to wash and scrub the crushers' feet first and rinse them in purified water, and that the crushing should be done in a cool place away from the heat of the summer sun, and that

EQUIPMENT LIST
(for 5 gallons of wine or
80–100 pounds of grapes)

- 10-gallon food grade plastic bucket or plastic garbage can
- Hydrometer with test jar (triple scale wine hydrometer)
- Acid Testing Kit
- Sulfite Test Kit
- Crusher or Stemmer-Crusher (can be rented)
- Press (can be rented) or can use cheesecloth
- Two 5-gallon glass carboys
- Funnel
- 2–3 fermentation locks
- #7 drilled rubber stopper
- Siphon assembly
- Thermometer
- Bottle filler
- Corker
- 25 wine corks
- 25 wine bottles
- Wine yeast (1 gram per gallon of must)
- Yeast nutrient
- Tartaric acid
- Sulfite

* Approximately 16 pounds of grapes will give 1 gallon of wine;
1 gallon of wine fills 5 standard wine bottles (mature vines
produce 8–12 pounds of fruit depending upon the variety)

After Crushing Red Grapes

Remove 90% of the larger stems and place the liquid mixture of juice, skins, pulp, and seeds—now called must—into a food-grade plastic garbage can. Cover lightly with a towel (to keep flies and other insects out) and place food-grade plastic garbage cans in a safe spot for 12–24 hours before adding yeast.

After Crushing White Grapes

Option I: Crush the berries and leave on the stems and skin anywhere from 2–16 hours. Add ½ ounce of pectin enzyme per 100 pounds of grapes in order to soften berries to yield more juice when it is time to press (optional). If fruit is very ripe, you should not need pectin. Cover lightly with a towel and store in a cool place (55–65 degrees Fahrenheit to avoid oxidation and browning) and leave for 2–16 hours. Press the must, funnel the juice into glass carboys, and let sit for 24 hours at room temperature before adding yeast. By leaving the juice on the skins, the wine is more susceptible to cloudiness; however, this technique will give a fuller-bodied taste with many more intense flavors.

Option II: Crush and stem the berries. Do not add pectin. Press the juice immediately. After pressing the juice (not called must since there are no skins, pulp, or seeds left), place in glass carboys and store at room temperature for 24 hours before adding yeast. This technique will produce a lighter, fruitier wine.

Testing Sugars and Acidity of Red or White Must and White Juice

Remove 1 pint of must or juice. If must, strain in order to produce about 6 ounces of juice. When testing the sugars, the temperature of the 6 ounces of juice should be anywhere from 55–75 degrees Fahrenheit. (If it is not, either warm or cool it to an acceptable level.) To warm must or juice: submerge the bowl with the 6 ounces of juice into another bowl filled with warm/hot water. To cool the must or juice: place a Ziploc bag full of ice into the mixture.

Sugar Test

Fill the test jar to the desired level and place the hydrometer into the juice. White wine should be anywhere from 20–27 degrees Brix (20–27%) and red wine anywhere from 22–27 degrees Brix (22–27%). The final alcohol level of the wine will be approximately half of the degrees Brix of the must or juice. (Optimal level is 12.5% alcohol, which would be 25 degrees Brix). To increase sugar levels add a sugar and water solution and test sugar levels again.

Acidity Test

Use TA kit (purchased from winemaking stores) in order to test acidity. Levels can run anywhere from .5–.9%. The advantage of higher acidity is that fermentation will remain clean, and the bad organisms will not be able to survive. The disadvantage is that the wine may be bitter and tart. For red wines, the best acid contents are from 0.65–0.80%, and for whites the best acid contents are 0.60–0.75%. To raise the acidity level, add tartaric acid at 1 teaspoon–1 gallon of must or juice. This will raise the level approximately 0.15%. To lower the acidity, dilute the must or juice by adding a sugar and water solution. One gallon of water and 4 1/2 cups of white sugar added to 5 gallons of must or juice will reduce the acidity by 0.14%.

pH Test

Use pH papers or a pH meter to test. Crushed must or juice should range from 3.0–4.0. Generally, fruit that is low in sugar is lower in pH (3.0) and higher in acidity, and fruit that is high in sugar will be higher in pH (4.0) and lower in acidity. Hence, a wine with lower pH will be stronger against spoilage because the acid levels are higher. Luckily, adjusting sugars and acidity will help make these figures closer to the desired numbers.

How to Sulfite the Must or Juice after Crush

Sulfite purifies and controls natural spoilage from microorganisms that turn wines into vinegar. And sulfite helps to sanitize and sterilize the liquid and kill off or stun wild yeast. If little mold was present on the grapes at the time of harvest a sulfur dioxide level of around 50 parts per million (ppm) is acceptable. If large amounts of mold were present at harvest the sulfur dioxide level can go up to 100 ppm. The easiest way to achieve this is to purchase Campden tablets from a local wine store supplier. One tablet for each gallon of must or juice will bring levels up to 50 ppm. (Before adding, smash tablet in small amount of warm water.)

300 pounds of grapes should take around twenty minutes to stomp. But the year I won the winemaking medal, no one washed their feet. The buckets of water for washing feet that were set out for my sixty or so guests were ignored, particularly by the twenty-five or so children that came to partake in the grape-squishing contest we held. The masses of children waiting in line to jump into my six- by eight-foot wooden vat full of freshly picked Cabernet Sauvignon grapes were only concerned with how purple their feet could get and who they could push to the floor of the slippery, juice-filled stomping box. And although we moved the grapes rapidly, directly from the vineyard into the stomping bin fifty yards from where we picked, the time of day was around 4:30 in the afternoon and we were working in the blistering hot sun of early September. And even though it should have taken a mere twenty or thirty minutes to stomp, it took nearly three hours. By the time we were finished the fruit was bruised and battered. We did it our way, and didn't copy anyone else's painting.

✳ ✳ ✳

In many of the winemaking classes I took we traveled around and interviewed famous enologists spread throughout Sonoma County. We talked to winemakers from Kenwood, Kunde, Geyser Peak, Seghesio, Martinelli, Dry Creek, Sonoma Cutrer, Ferarri Carano, Rafanelli, and a host of others. Some winemakers said to use wild yeasts and others said you must inoculate with yeast, and some said punch down the must every four to six hours and others said once a day, and some said sulfite to levels of 25 ppm and others said 60 ppm and still others said don't sulfite at all. My head was spinning because there were no consistencies or established norms.

Help, I thought, I'm gonna flunk the winemaking test if I don't get a concrete recipe. But there was no such thing.

"Winemaking is not for those who need exact recipes to follow," one winemaker said after I demanded a concrete formula. I soon learned that for every step of the process there are sixteen (or more) equally successful and different ways to do it. For instance, my Cabernet Sauvignon that won the bronze medal was made with oak, but it wasn't essence of oak drops, and it wasn't aged in oak barrels (as most big wineries do); instead, it was from a piece of oak that my husband bought at Home Depot.

"You have to have elements of oak in the wine; it will enhance the flavor," Chuck told me a winemaker friend told him.

"Yes, Chuck," I said, "but not oak from Home Depot." Something must have gotten lost in the translation. "I think your winemaker friend meant for us to age the wine in toasted oak barrels," I argued. I envisioned it to be like adding essence of lemon to homemade lemonade in order to heighten the flavor. But no, I ended up with the economical version: a piece of oak Chuck purchased in the lumber department from Home Depot that he sawed and whittled away to a size that would fit into our cheap five-gallon glass carboys.

I'll never forget how happy he seemed in his worn sweats and dirty t-shirt as he banged away on that piece of Home Depot wood. He spent hours in the freezing fall weather, steam rising from his mouth as he breathed heavily and sanded away at remnants of the wood. I was later shocked when he put the piece of oak strip in my oven, turned on the heat and, as he said, "Toasted it to perfection—like a perfectly roasted marshmallow."

"I hate marshmallows," I replied, increasingly annoyed by his contribution to the process. Somehow, his toasting technique did not fit my romantic vision of how oak flavors should be instilled in wine. I dreamed of beautiful European cellars with curing oak barrels that were carved with intricate scrollwork, filled with aging wine. Cellars filled with wine that would capture complex oak flavors from the glamorous environment and the traditional, old barrels. Instead, I had to settle for a curing environment that was reminiscent of a new cooking recipe gone awry. I complained that our whole house smelled like a wood factory, but Chuck ignored me. Days into the process, he handed me a strip of wood with charred black marks running horizontally through the grain. The piece of oak looked bad and smelled bad, and my oven was never the same. But I smiled and graciously accepted the rather unconventional gift. "Thanks," I grunted, trying to sound appreciative. He later told me that he was thrilled to be handling this part of the process, the part that he thought was the most important. He may have been right.

WHAT TYPE OF YEAST IS THE BEST TO USE?

Different types of yeast produce slightly different results. Some wine supply stores will carry only one type and others will carry many different types. Listed below are a few of the subtle differences between wine yeast. Remember that simply because a certain strain comes from a certain region does not mean that your wine will taste like the wine from that region.

Prise de Mosse (Epernay)

Normally used for white wines. Considered to be a fast fermenter at temperatures between 50–77 degrees Fahrenheit and has the ability to produce high alcohol levels. Not much flavor.

Epernay II

Best for fruity wines, and mostly whites. Slow to moderate fermenter at temperatures between 50–80 degrees Fahrenheit. Produces fruity flavors.

Montrachet

Good for both red and white wine. Can withstand high SO_2 levels and is considered to be a moderate fermenter at temperatures between 59–80 degrees Fahrenheit. Produces complex flavors.

Pasteur Champagne

Can restart a fermentation and is used for both red and white wine. Produces a fast fermentation, dry flavor, and high alcohol levels at temperatures between 59–80 degrees Fahrenheit. Not much flavor.

Simi White (French White)

Good for Chardonnay and dry white wines. A slow fermenter at temperatures between 55–85 degrees Fahrenheit. Produces fruity flavors.

Rhone

Good for Rhone Varietals, Zinfandel, and Petite Sirah. A moderate fermenter with high alcohol levels at temperatures between 59–82 degrees Fahrenheit. Produces a fruity flavor.

Steinburg

Good for Gewürtztraminer and Riesling. Low to moderate fermenter at temperatures between 40–70 degrees Fahrenheit. Produces fruity and spicy flavors.

When I received my ratings from the wine judges one of the descriptions about the wine read, "Lovely, smoky flavor that resembles a burning oak field with a whisper of mustard grass." No one described the flavor as down-to-earth, economical, and innovative with a hint of Home Depot and a touch of gas characteristic of a General Electric oven.

Imperfect environment was again my situation during one fermentation. Not only did all family members feel compelled to sample and touch the bubbling liquid, so too did the birds. I learned the hard way that my fermenting red must, stored in my garage, was a great attraction for the birds. One particular day I had forgotten to cover my plastic garbage can with a towel—big mistake. In the night I heard bird noises coming from my garage. I ran out screaming in an attempt to get rid of them. The birds were drunk from the half-fermented juice and were diving in all directions. I climbed into my car, seeking refuge from their onslaught, and spent the better part of the night waiting for them to figure their way out of the wide-open garage.

Fermentation is a process not easily disturbed—even by birds. The grapes miraculously turn into wine, and it occurs whether you want it to or not. The yeast cells that are present on the grape skins take control and the sugar molecules form juices that are broken down into alcohol and carbon dioxide, which are then released as a toxic gas. During this process there are many stages that produce reactions and byproducts.

There are microorganisms, yeasts, and bacteria, present at the start of the fermentation process, needed to help continue the steps that eventually produce wine. The time it takes to complete fermentation, or in simple terms, to convert all of the available sugar into alcohol, is dependent upon fermentation temperature, amount of yeast, and yeast nutrients. By adding sulfites and inoculating with one certain type of yeast, that specific yeast becomes the dominant one while the wild yeasts play a necessary, but secondary role. There is controversy about whether or not yeast inoculation is really necessary. For warmer places probably so, since an overgrowth of spoilage organisms, due to warmer temperatures, may produce harmful effects on the necessary growth of wild yeasts for fermentation. Yet, for cooler regions encouraging the wild or natural yeast flora is a more simplistic and natural way to produce the wine. Wild yeasts on grapes can be encouraged by picking a group of healthy, ripe grapes (approximately one week before harvest) and crushing them in a bowl. After about a week there will be a full fermentation started with the natural yeast flora, and this can be added to the must or juice when ready to start the fermentation process.

Winemaking can be challenging. From my earliest remembrances of where wine came from—the days when my family took stabs at making homegrown wine, and when my dad unleashed a storage spot for his wine by digging an eight- by ten-foot hole into the earth of our basement wall, carefully placing a rickety wooden door with a padlock over it (to mimic the way the French did it, he said)—to today, after ten plus years of toiling and sweating to perfect my grape-growing and winemaking, the challenge has continued to present itself in various ways. Nowadays I tell my father that the French wouldn't have locked their wine cellar doors; they would have left them unlocked for all to see. "Yes," he grins, "but if I had done that I wouldn't have seen many of my wines reach their perfect age." He's referring to the time after I'd graduated from Berkeley and

ADDING YEAST TO ENCOURAGE FERMENTATION

Red Must

Add one 5-gram packet of yeast (purchased at winemaking shop) for every 5 gallons. Spread yeast across top of must in plastic garbage can or bucket and after 8–10 hours stir into must or grow the yeast in sweet juice or diluted wine. When 1/2 of sugar in juice or wine has fermented, stir into must. Once must has formed cap (grape skins come to the surface) it needs to be punched down with clean hands or arms at least twice a day. When Brix reading reaches 0–4 degrees, it is time to press the must. Use clean bucket and cheesecloth or rent a grape press. Fermentation of must temperatures for red wines should begin between 60–70 degrees Fahrenheit and progress to around 80–85 degrees Fahrenheit. After pressing, the last part of fermentation temperature should be around 65–70 degrees Fahrenheit.

White Juice

Siphon off the lees into a clean carboy, or ferment with juice left on lees. Add one 5-gram packet of yeast and 1 ounce of yeast nutrient for every 100 pounds of grapes (there are 75–80 pounds of grapes in one 5-gallon glass carboy). Fill carboy 3/4 full (to allow for expansion once fermentation begins). Attach fermentation lock. Fermentation temperature is best between 55–65 degrees Fahrenheit. Fermentation should begin within 12–24 hours and should last anywhere from 5 days to 3 weeks. Monitor progress by taking degree Brix readings using hydrometer.

How To Deal with Stuck Fermentation

If liquid does not start to froth and grow after a couple of days, the fermentation may be stuck.

LOW TEMPERATURES

Remove a bucket of the must or juice and heat it up by placing it in a sink filled with hot water. Pour it back on top of red must and leave for two hours. Stir in and the fermentation process will begin.

HIGH TEMPERATURES

Temperatures of must or juice need to remain below 90 degrees Fahrenheit. To cool down the must or juice place a Ziploc bag filled with ice cubes directly into the liquid.

When Is Fermentation Over?

A chromatography kit purchased from the wine supply store can be used to test for ended fermentation or taste the liquid or test the acidity periodically and once the numbers begin to stabilize this will mean the fermentation process is over. Once complete, wait 2–3 weeks longer, then begin racking.

Racking

To be done after all visible signs of fermentation are complete, meaning no more bubbles or frothing. At first racking, some winemakers fine the wine by adding an agent called Bentonite or Sparkolloid. This is not necessary, but it can help clarify the liquid. Racking means siphoning the top layer of liquid from the undesirable solids and used yeast cells. This step helps purify the wine. Place the wine-filled carboy on a table and the clean carboy below. Use a 1/2-inch food-grade hose and submerge it 2 inches into the wine. Suck the wine through the other end of the hose, and just before it reaches your mouth, place it into the clean carboy. Pull the hose out of the carboy before it reaches the sediment. Fill the carboy to the top so unwanted microorganisms don't get in (add store-bought wine if doesn't reach top), and stopper with an airlock. At the end of fermentation, and at each racking, sulfite can be added to bring level up to 20 ppm (2 Campden tablets for each 5-gallon carboy). For best clarifying, the wine can be racked 4–5 times before bottling. During the aging process it is best to store wine in area with temperatures anywhere from 50–60 degrees Fahrenheit.

Bottling

The free sulfite content should be tested and levels should be brought to 30 ppm. Siphon the wine into sterilized bottles, cork, and store at temperatures anywhere from 50–60 degrees Fahrenheit.

I came home hoping to find my parents around so that we could celebrate. They weren't home, so I went to Dad's nifty wine cellar—with the 1970s-style wooden bar he'd built—and grabbed a bottle of wine, that looked like a simple bottle, and toasted myself in the dark atmosphere of our homemade wine cellar.

"What the hell...." he said matter-of-factly when he and my mother came home from dinner. "You drank my Duckhorn Cabernet."

"Sorry, Dad," I said, "it looked like it wasn't anything too serious, and it had a duck on the label that was really cute." He forgave me, I'm sure thinking that I knew all along that it was a great bottle of wine. I really didn't.

Many years after my family's attempt at winemaking I asked my mom about what kind of yeast they used, and if they added sulfites to the wine.

"Yeast? We had no idea we were supposed to add yeast and sulfite to the wine."

"That was your problem, Mom," I said laughing. It now makes sense to me why their wine tasted like a dead fish from the bottom of a green lake.

Attempting to make wine and following the winemaking processes requires knowledge. Certain rituals need to be painstakingly followed or else the wine will end up tasting like dirty socks, dead fish, and remnants of angry nature. Wine spoils easily if certain steps are not realized, and large amounts of it can be wasted and lost—even if the processes are done accurately. The first time my family and I racked our own wine, we didn't have the siphon hose set up at the appropriate angle. Dude sucked and sucked and sucked away on the rubbery hose until he was red in the face. Then Chuck took over, adjusted the angle of the carboys and the hose, and the juice came with such force that he not only swallowed half of what had just circulated through the hose, but what he couldn't swallow spilled out all over the ground. The dog lapped it up and went to lay in the sun. I ran around in circles swearing and screaming about the loss of wine they had all just caused me. But the wine was good, even after all the mistakes we had made. We followed the basic recipe and only deviated when we felt creatively inclined.

Finishing the winemaking process is always cause for a celebration—no matter how many mistakes you make along the way. Last year after harvest I said to Chuck, "Isn't this just the most exciting time of year?" We were heading east from Glen Ellen along Highway 12 to Sonoma to spend the evening celebrating with six other home winemaking couples to commemorate the end of harvest. Leaving Glen Ellen we passed the European-looking wooden signs that point to Wellington Vineyards, Stone Creek, Benziger, Kenwood, Matanzas Creek, and Kunde, and passed Arrowood, B.R. Cohen, Valley of the Moon, and Carmenet heading toward Sebastiani, Buena Vista, Ravenswood, and Gundlach-Bundschu; our final destination was Castle Road in Sonoma. Once there, we feasted until two in the morning on dishes that each couple had made, many of which included ingredients they had grown or hunted themselves—wild chanterelle mushrooms spread over baguettes, red pepper soup, boeuf à la bourguignonne, organic green salad, pasta with fresh shrimp, elk and layered potato soufflé, and decadent chocolate cake. The wine was made and came from the wine cellars of all of the guests: Riesling, Sangiovese, Merlot, Cabernet, Pinot Noir, Zinfandel. I stopped counting after a while, it was so dramatic. The conversation was lively as we talked about our wines, many of them medal winners, and laughed about how inspiring it is to grow grapes and make wine; how it captivates and stays in your memory like a sparkling jewel; how it interposes with your life and makes the anticipation of each new season worthwhile; how it brightens your spirit and cleanses your soul. Cheers! A votre Santé! Bottoms up! ¡Salud! we said, as we finished off the last drops of wine and the final morsels of food.

On the way home I thought (a little unclear after all of the food and drink) there's just nothing like the Machiavellian trap of Sonoma wine country during winemaking season; it's crafty, cunning, and illusive. The whole valley exudes memories of social gatherings, and one can wile away their days thinking that they are amidst a circus of good cheer, that they are encircled by a jovial party with flowing wine and absorbing chat, and that they are amongst good friends at a sweet-smelling garden party filled with goodies and drink. This is a two-faced façade that exists only in the mind. When I first came to this valley—until I learned about the guile of this masquerade—I actually suspected friends of drinking wine during the early hours of the day. But this was an untrue myth. I realized that the smell of wine in Sonoma clearly dominates the air—not the breath of its inhabitants—and these smells are merely just another will-o'-the-wisp that comes with this serene land at the end of harvest.

A great bottle of wine paired with a savory meal is a creative end to an enlightening and moving beginning.

GLOSSARY OF WINEMAKING TERMS

Brix: Measurement of the percentage of sugar present in must or wine.

Cap: When primary fermentation occurs, the solid matter comes to the surface and forms a barrier over the liquid. The liquid below the cap bubbles away indicating that the yeast is working to convert the sugars to alcohol and carbon dioxide.

Carboy: A 5-gallon glass bottle (used mostly by home winemakers) with a wide bottom and a narrow neck. Used to store red wine for secondary fermentation before bottling, and for white wine after pressing.

Crushing and Stemming: The process of removing stems from grapes after the skins are broken in the act of crushing the fruit. It can be done with feet and hands, or with a stemmer-crusher.

Fermentation: The actual process of adding or encouraging yeast to convert the sugar to carbon dioxide and alcohol.

Primary Fermentation: The first part of fermentation where two-thirds of the sugar is converted to alcohol. Usually this takes about 1–3 weeks from the time the yeast is added or encouraged.

Secondary Fermentation: The final conversion of sugars to alcohol after wine has been pressed and is no longer exposed to air.

Fermentation Lock: A stopper that allows the carbon dioxide produced from the process of fermentation, to escape from the container without allowing air to enter.

Hydrometer: A piece of equipment that measures the gravity of grapes, must, or wine. This allows for a reading of sugar percent to be achieved.

Lees: Sediment composed of used yeast cells and other solids that remain after fermentation.

Must: The liquid mixture of juice, skins, pulp, and seeds that is achieved after stemming and crushing, but before pressing.

pH: Indicates the level of acidity that will be produced in the wine.

Pressing: Must is pressed by using a wine press, or straining through cheesecloth. The juice is removed from the skins and seeds. For white wine the pressing is normally done immediately after crush, and for red wine the pressing is done after primary fermentation.

Punching Down: Should be done twice a day using clean arms, or a piece of clean wood, during primary fermentation. The cap needs to be broken up and then mixed. This helps evenly distribute the yeast so that fermentation can continue. Punching down also helps insure good color for the wine because the liquid below the cap is mixed in with the solid masses allowing more color to be extracted from the skins.

Racking: After fermentation the wine is separated from the used yeast cells. Siphon the layer of clear wine away to help purify the liquid.

Refractometer: A more expensive version of the hydrometer that can be used to measure the sugar percentages in the grapes before harvest.

Sulfur Dioxide (SO$_2$): Add after crush (and before fermentation) to must in the form of potassium metabisulfite crystals or Campden tablets. SO$_2$ kills or controls unwanted yeast at fermentation, prevents oxidation, and controls overgrowth of organisms at racking and bottling.

Titratable Acidity(TA): Can be determined by a process called titration. TA refers to malic acid and tartaric acid as well as traces of other acids. For purposes of acid testing, tartaric acid is the acid measured.

Yeast: Found naturally on grape skins, or specific strains purchased from winemaking stores. The yeast is necessary for converting sugars in the grapes to alcohol. Additions of yeast help to insure consistent and complete fermentation.

Wild Yeast: Natural yeast found on grape skins.

Yeast Nutrient: Can be added as extra "food" for the yeast.

SYNOPSIS

Seasons Among the Vines: Life Lessons from the California Wine Country and Paris

The second edition of *Seasons Among the Vines* has added enlightening pieces of the international world of wine exposing some of the most riveting old world style secrets to the new world. After spending nearly ten years of her life rebuilding her world after her husband is killed in a car accident and three days before the release of her first edition of *Seasons Among the Vines* in 2003, Paula Moulton decides to embark on an enchanting and courageous adventure enrolling in a ten-month wine management program with twenty other international students in the pilot wine program at Le Cordon Bleu in Paris. Leaving her home in Sonoma as her third and last child goes off to college, she not only faces the struggles of living in a foreign country, but experiences the rigors of the French academic system complete with a one month stint in Bergerac as a cellar rat and a six-week internship as a sommelier in a prestigious restaurant off Le Champs Elysees. This second edition of *Seasons Among the Vines* is spunky and informative; interspersed throughout is still advice for weekend gardeners and wine-loving suburbanites on how to make wine at home, but Moulton has not only added everything a reader could ever need to know about how to smell, swirl, and taste wine, but all the ins and outs to successful food and wine pairing, and how to make intelligent decisions when choosing wine. From international escapades, to unforeseen wine disasters, to trial and error with food and wine pairing, events both amusing and rueful make for a bona fide picture of what it means to follow a dream even after suffering great loss.

ABOUT THE AUTHOR

© photo credit

Paula Moulton is co-founder and CEO of A Sip Away. She is a viticulturist, award-winning winemaker, and published author with over 25 years of experience in the wine industry. She has worked with wine talent such as Joel Peterson of Ravenswood Winery, Mike Benziger of Benziger Family Winery, Jean-Luc Thunevin (Bordeaux's Bad Boy wine), and Phil Coturri of Enterprise Vineyards. She was recently one of 20 students invited to spend a year in Paris, France studying wine management at Le Cordon Bleu. Paula has appeared on the Today Show, CBS, NBC, ABC, FOX, CRN, and other major media outlets as an author and wine industry leader. She holds a BA from UC Berkeley in Rhetoric, an AS in viticulture from Santa Rosa Junior College, and a Wine Management degree from Le Cordon Bleu, Paris, France. She currently lives in Sonoma, California.

ACKNOWLEDGMENTS

Without my three children, Ashley, Christopher, and Alexandra, this second edition of *Seasons Among the Vines* would not exist. I am blessed to have them as my children and to be the recipient of the hope, inspiration, and strength they gave me, which allowed me to carry on with my dreams and take on Paris alone after the death of their father. You are my Angels.

To my then fiancé and now husband, Dr. Stephen Paul Bowne, and his children, Christian and Bretton: Thank you for letting me be unencumbered for a year so I could continue my pursuit of viticulture and wine and—most of all—take that exorbitant leap of faith that comes with fear, adventure, and the need to pursue a stolen dream. I am forever indebted to your hardiness and willingness to let me follow my intentions.

To Monsieur Ramage, the heart and soul of my success and the most dedicated wine professor that I could have ever dreamed of spending a year with: you have touched the hearts of many students—most of all mine.

Thanks to B. Preston who made me laugh through countless hours of education, and to Le Cordon Bleu Paris for initiating the pilot program of Le Cordon Bleu 2012 Wine Management, the core reason that I went to Paris . . . alone.

Thanks also to my dearest friends in Paris—BBC Girl, Pilot Girl, New Baby Girl, Texan Boy, Singapore Girl, Swan Girl, Australian Girl, Finnish Lady, Turkish Girl, and French Girl—for helping me cope and teaching me that we are all in this together, no matter where we come from.

To my family and literary friends—Kenneth Clark, Karol Clark, Paige Locke, and Phyllis Hatfield—thank you for being there from the beginning.

To Megan and Michael Janis, Megan Burns and David Greenberg, Jeff and Judy Lopes, and Rachel LeFort: thank you for coming to Paris when I was homesick and feeling lost.

Thanks to Kirsten Melton, for the original title of *Seasons* and because France was not as easy without you.

Thanks to my WillMar family, who got me through my grief and made me who I am today.

Thanks to She Writes Press and the women of She Writes, who support each other in the ongoing process of writing and communicating the written word.

And thank you to Brooke Warner, a visionary and spiritual leader, who has always been there for me with open arms and literary sustenance.

Finally, this book is in memory of Dr. Charles Wade Moulton, who is in heaven among the Angels, just sitting atop the clouds and clapping in gratitude.

SELECTED TITLES FROM SHE WRITES PRESS

She Writes Press is an independent publishing company founded to serve women writers everywhere. Visit us at www.shewritespress.com.

Tasting Home: Coming of Age in the Kitchen by Judith Newton. $16.95, 978-1-938314-03-2. An extraordinary journey through the cuisines, cultures, and politics of the 1940s through 2011, complete with recipes.

Hedgebrook Cookbook: Celebrating Radical Hospitality by Denise Barr & Julie Rosten. $24.95, 978-1-938314-22-3. Delectable recipes and inspiring writing, straight from Hedgebrook's farmhouse table to yours.

Away from the Kitchen: Untold Stories, Private Menus, Guarded Recipes, and Insider Tips by Dawn Blume Hawkes. $24.95, 978-1-938314-36-0. A food book for those who want it all: the menus, the recipes, and the behind-the-scenes scoop on some of America's favorite chefs.

Americashire: A Field Guide to a Marriage by Jennifer Richardson. $15.95, 978-1-938314-30-8. A couple's decision about whether or not to have a child plays out against the backdrop of their new home in the English countryside.

Splitting the Difference: A Heart-Shaped Memoir by Tré Miller-Rodríguez. $19.95, 978-1-938314-20-9. When 34-year-old Tré Miller-Rodríguez's husband dies suddenly from a heart attack, her grief sends her on an unexpected journey that culminates in a reunion with the biological daughter she gave up at 18.

Seeing Red: A Woman's Quest for Truth, Power, and the Sacred by Lone Morch. $16.95, 978-1-938314-12-4. One woman's journey over inner and outer mountains—a quest that takes her to the holy Mt. Kailas in Tibet, through a seven-year marriage, and into the arms of the fierce goddess Kali, where she discovers her powerful, feminine self.

CPSIA information can be obtained at www.ICGtesting.com
Printed in the USA
LVOW11s1049221213

366349LV00003B/3/P